IMAGES OF THE
NATIONAL ARCHIVES

CODEBREAKERS

IMAGES OF THE
NATIONAL ARCHIVES
CODEBREAKERS

STEPHEN TWIGGE

PEN & SWORD
HISTORY

AN IMPRINT OF PEN & SWORD BOOKS LTD.
YORKSHIRE - PHILADELPHIA

First published in Great Britain in 2020 by
Pen and Sword History
An imprint of
Pen & Sword Books Ltd
Yorkshire - Philadelphia

ISBN 978 1 52673 080 0

The National Archives is the official archives and publisher for the UK Government, and for England and Wales. We work to bring together and secure the future of the public record, both digital and physical, for future generations.

The National Archives is open to all, offering a range of activities and spaces to enjoy, as well as our reading rooms for research. Many of our most popular records are also available online.

A CIP catalogue record for this book is available from the British Library.

Typeset in Minion Pro 11/14.5 by
Aura Technology and Software Services, India.

Printed and bound in the UK by CPI Group (UK) Ltd., Croydon, CR0 4YY.

Pen & Sword Books Ltd incorporates the Imprints of Pen & Sword Books Archaeology, Atlas, Aviation, Battleground, Discovery, Family History, History, Maritime, Military, Naval, Politics, Railways, Select, Transport, True Crime, Fiction, Frontline Books, Leo Cooper, Praetorian Press, Seaforth Publishing, Wharncliffe and White Owl.

For a complete list of Pen & Sword titles please contact

PEN & SWORD BOOKS LIMITED
47 Church Street, Barnsley, South Yorkshire, S70 2AS, England
E-mail: enquiries@pen-and-sword.co.uk
Website: www.pen-and-sword.co.uk

or

PEN AND SWORD BOOKS
1950 Lawrence Rd, Havertown, PA 19083, USA
E-mail: Uspen-and-sword@casematepublishers.com
Website: www.penandswordbooks.com

CONTENTS

Introduction...6

Chapter 1:   The Secret Office and Room 40.............................8
Chapter 2:   The Government Code and Cypher School.......34
Chapter 3:   Ultra Goes to War...55
Chapter 4:   The Battle of the Atlantic...................................85
Chapter 5:   The War in the Far East.......................................96
Chapter 6:   Alan Turing..107
Chapter 7:   Post War Developments.....................................117

Further Reading...129
Index..130

INTRODUCTION

The story of Allied codebreaking during the Second World War is one of industry, intrigue and invention. The centre of Britain's codebreaking operation was located at Bletchley Park in rural Buckinghamshire. It was from here, a nineteenth century mansion in the British countryside, that a hastily assembled army of codebreakers battled to decipher Germany's secret wartime communications. From the invasion of Poland in September 1939 to the fall of Japan in August 1945, a motley collection of linguists, mathematicians and crossword enthusiasts pitted their combined wits against the 'unbreakable' naval Enigma codes and Lorenz ciphers used by Hitler and the German High Command. The deciphered high-level signals intelligence disseminated to military commanders was known as Ultra and had a major influence on the outcome of the war, most notably contributing to crucial successes in the battle for the Atlantic and providing critical information on troop positions in Normandy before the Allied invasion began on 6 June 1944.

Propaganda postcard featuring Winston Churchill complete with Tommy Gun. *CN 11/6*

Britain's interest in codes and ciphers pre-dates the Second World War and possesses a proud heritage stretching back to the court of Elizabeth I and her spymaster Sir Francis Walsingham. This book traces the history of British codebreaking from the school for espionage established by Walsingham in the 1570s to the work of the Secret Office of the Post Office in the eighteenth century to the creation of the Government Code and Cypher School in 1919. The exploits of the two world wars form a major aspect of the story and include the achievements of the Admiralty's 'Room 40' and the infamous Zimmermann telegram, the breaking of Enigma code and the critical importance of Ultra in the battle of the Atlantic and the war in the Far East. The contribution made by Alan Turing and his ground-breaking work into computing is also described and his influence on future generations is assessed. The book ends with a brief overview of post war developments and the importance of signals intelligence in the Cold War.

Following the end of the Second World War, Churchill ordered that all evidence relating to codebreaking be destroyed. Individuals who had worked at Bletchley Park were required to sign the Official Secrets Act and explicitly instructed not to divulge any detail of the work they had undertaken at Bletchley Park, even to their families. Despite this draconian edict, many documents, including internal histories, intelligence reports and copies of decrypts did survive and were eventually transferred to the National Archives at Kew. Key documents from the archive are faithfully reproduced in this book and provide a fascinating insight into Britain's cryptographic secrets of the Second World War. These documents are supplemented by additional material highlighting Britain's rich history in codes and ciphers. The collection covers three centuries of the nation's history and demonstrates the centrality of signals intelligence for the conduct of British statecraft. Brought together for the first time, this book enables readers to explore these remarkable and momentous records for themselves.

CHAPTER 1

THE SECRET OFFICE AND ROOM 40

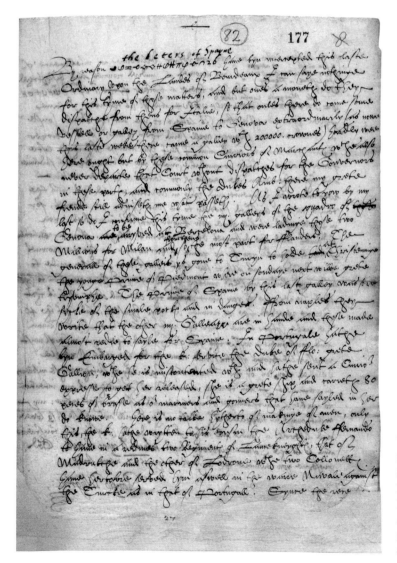

Two page intelligence
report by Anthony
Standen, alias
Pompeo Pelligrini, to
Francis Walsingham
concerning events
in Florence 1587.
SP 94/2 pt2 (1)

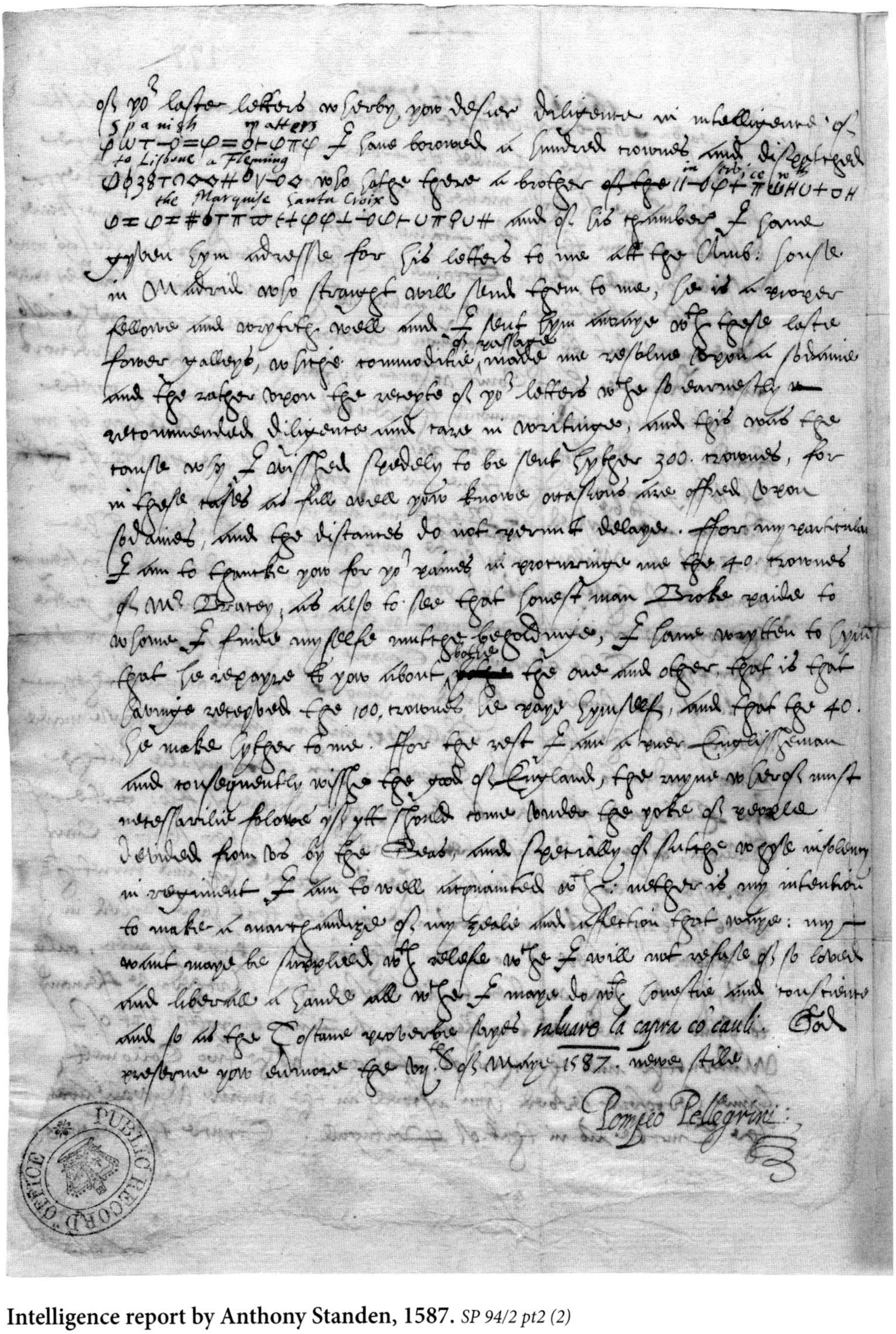

Intelligence report by Anthony Standen, 1587. *SP 94/2 pt2 (2)*

Britain has a long tradition of breaking codes and ciphers and intercepting the communications of foreign powers. During the sixteenth century, monarchs, ministers and ambassadors often established cipher offices and employed cipher secretaries to encrypt diplomatic and military correspondence. In England, the safety of Elizabeth I was constantly under threat from her enemies at home and abroad. In response, Elizabeth's Secretary of State, Sir Francis Walsingham created a school for espionage in London in the 1570s, recruiting spies and codebreakers and establishing a network of agents and informants throughout Europe. In the seventeenth century, the Post Office maintained a Secret Office tasked with intercepting the mail of suspected plotters who had 'wicked designs' against the Commonwealth. To break the secret codes of those countries plotting against British interests overseas, a deciphering department was established. Housed in a series of rooms next to the Foreign Office in Whitehall, the Secret Office was staffed by Isaac Dorislaus, a Dutch linguist and legal adviser to the High Court of Justice, and Dr John Wallis, a mathematician and clergyman widely regarded as the most influential English mathematician before Newton. The Secret Office had two primary functions: to provide codes and ciphers to enable secure and reliable communication with British officials overseas; and to covertly intercept and read coded messages from abroad.

The difference between a code and a cipher is that in a coded message the original words or letters are substituted for a random string of letters derived from a codebook. In a cipher, a message is encrypted using a complex mathematical equation known as an algorithm. Wallis's knowledge of mathematics enabled him to develop complex algorithms making his ciphers virtually unbreakable. In 1703, Wallis was succeeded in his post by his grandson, William Blencowe, who was appointed as the government's first official decipherer. The existence of the Secret Office was first made public in 1742 following the downfall of Sir Robert Walpole and the subsequent investigation into the misappropriation of public funds. It was discovered that in the ten years between 1732 and 1742, the Post Office had received £45,675 to fund its secret activities. John Barbutt, the Head of the Post Office was summoned to parliament for questioning. Papers in the National Archives show that Barbutt – questioned under oath – revealed that the allowance was used to fund a Secret Office responsible for the interception and inspection of foreign correspondence under the direction of the Secretary of State. The disclosure of the Secret Office alerted foreign powers that their communications were being routinely intercepted. They therefore changed their ciphers or delivered important messages by courier so depriving Britain of a valuable source of secret intelligence.

Ciphers used by Mary Queen of Scots in the 1580s. *SP 53/22 f1*

Babington's acknowledgement of ciphers used in correspondence with Mary Queen of Scots, September 1586. *SP 12/193 (54)*

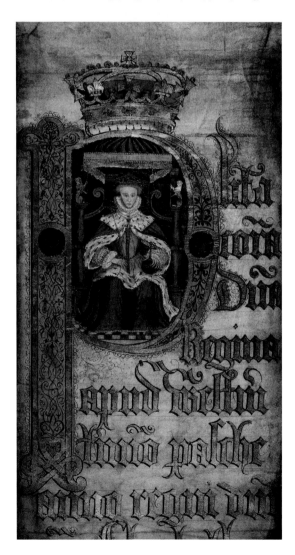

Mary Queen of Scots ciphers, 1580s (detail 1). *SP 53/22 f1*

Illuminated Coram Rege Roll showing Elizabeth I. *KB 27/1289/2*

15

The Numericall Alphabet

A	B	C	D	E	F	G	H	I	K	L	M	N	O	P	Q	R	S	T	V	W	X	Y	Z	a	b	c	d	e	f	g	h	i	k
8	10	13	12	11	9	7	6	19	16	4	2	1	14	17	27	30	33	32	31	29	18	26	25	20	21	22	23	24	18	15	5	3	34

1	2	3	4	5	6	7	8	9	10	11	12	13	14	15	16	17	18	19	20	21	22	23	24	25	26	27	28	29	30	31	32	33	34
N	M	i	L	h	A	G	A	J	B	E	D	C	O	g	K	P	J	a	b	c	d	e	z	y	L	x	W	R	J	S	k		

Private Marks for Names or words

receive	77	84	Mr Wm Godolphin	91	103	King	35	56
Letter	78	85	S: Wm Temple	92	104	Queen	36	57
Pacquett	79	86	Parliament	93	105	Duke	37	58
Post	80	87	Privy Councell	94	106	Prince	38	59
returne	81	88	Intelligence	95	107	Lord	39	60
Lady	82	89	Peace	96	108	Arlington	40	61
Consent magna	83	90	Treaty	97	109	Ye Keeper	41	62
			League	98	110	S: Rob Southwell	42	63
			Ea: of Sandwich	99	111	Dutch	43	64
			Court	100	112	french	44	65
			instruction	101	113	France	45	66
			F.B. Gascoign	102	114	Dane	46	67
						Suede	47	68
						Portugall	48	69
						Spayne	49	70
						Ambassadeur	50	71
						Flanders	51	72
						Holland	52	73
						England	53	74
						Scotland	54	75
						Ireland	55	76

CLAVIS UNIVERSALIS

```
 1 | 1
 2 | 2 1
 3 | 1 3 2
 4 | 1 3 2 4
 5 | 1 3 2 4 5
 6 | 1 3 4 6 5 2
 7 | 0 7 1 2 3 4 5
 8 | 8 7 4 1 2 3 5 6
 9 | 4 3 1 2 5 6 9 7 8
10 | 6 1 7 2 8 3 9 4 10 5
11 | 11 10 9 8 7 6 5 4 3 2 1
12 | 10 9 8 7 6 5 4 3 2 1 11 12
13 | 12 13 11 9 7 5 3 1 2 4 6 8 10
14 | 12 10 8 5 3 1 2 4 7 6 9 11 13 14
15 | 12 14 15 4 1 2 3 5 6 7 8 9 10 11 12
16 | 16 15 14 13 1 2 3 4 5 6 7 8 9 10 11 12
17 | 3 1 2 4 6 7 8 5 11 10 9 12 14 15 17 16
18 | 1 3 2 7 5 6 7 9 10 8 11 13 12 15 17 16 15 14
19 | 3 1 2 4 5 6 7 8 10 11 9 12 14 13 15 17 16 19 18
20 | 1 3 4 2 20 19 5 18 6 7 17 16 8 15 16 9 11 14 12 13
21 | 3 2 1 4 5 6 7 8 9 10 11 20 19 18 17 11 12 13 14 15 16
22 | 6 7 8 9 10 11 12 13 14 15 16 17 19 20 5 4 3 2 1
23 | 11 10 9 8 7 6 5 4 3 2 1 15 16 17 18 19 20 21 22 23 14 13 12
24 | 19 20 21 22 23 24 17 11 8 5 4 1 2 3 6 7 9 10 12 14 15 10 15 18
25 | 17 19 12 11 1 2 3 4 5 6 7 8 9 10 15 16 17 18 19 21 22 20 23 24 25
26 | 13 12 11 10 9 8 7 6 5 4 3 2 1 14 15 16 17 18 19 21 20 23 22 24 16 25
27 | 9 10 11 12 13 14 15 16 17 18 19 20 21 22 23 24 25 26 17 1 2 3 4 5 6 7 8
28 | 10 11 12 13 14 15 16 17 18 1 2 3 4 5 6 7 8 9 19 20 21 22 23 24 25 26 27 28
29 | 8 7 0 5 4 1 2 3 9 10 11 12 13 14 15 16 17 18 19 20 21 22 23 24 25 26 17 29 18
30 | 4 3 2 1 6 5 7 8 9 11 10 12 13 16 15 14 17 19 18 21 20 30 29 22 23 24 25 26 27 28
31 | 18 17 16 15 14 13 12 11 10 9 1 2 3 4 5 6 7 8 19 21 20 22 24 23 25 17 26 19 28 30 31
32 | 2 4 6 8 10 12 14 16 18 20 22 24 26 29 18 17 30 31 32 25 23 21 19 17 15 13 11 9 7 5 3 1
33 | 13 14 15 19 17 16 18 33 7 8 9 6 5 4 1 2 3 12 11 10 20 21 22 23 24 25 26 27 28 29 32 31 30
34 | 9 10 8 11 12 13 17 16 15 14 19 18 1 2 3 4 5 6 7 20 21 26 19 30 31 24 25 26 32 33 34 23 21 22
```

Numerical Alphabet Cipher used by British Secretaries of State 1660-85. *SP 106/6*

The Napoleonic wars that followed the French Revolution of 1789 ushered in a new era of bloodshed and intrigue and demonstrated the need for prompt and accurate field intelligence. The commander of British forces on the continent, the Duke of Wellington, readily appreciated its value and established a network of intelligence officers and local agents throughout Europe. These provided him with both strategic information, gathered by the interception of enemy letters, and tactical intelligence gathered by men in the field known as army guides. Wellington's chief codebreaker was George Scovell, a gifted linguist who served in the Intelligence Branch as Deputy Assistant Quartermaster-General. The value of intercepted communications was readily demonstrated during the Peninsular War of 1808-1814 when Scovell cracked the French Army's *Grande Chiffre*, a cipher derived from a mid-eighteenth century diplomatic code based on 1400 numbers with meaningless figures added to the end of letters. In December 1812, Scovell deciphered an intercepted

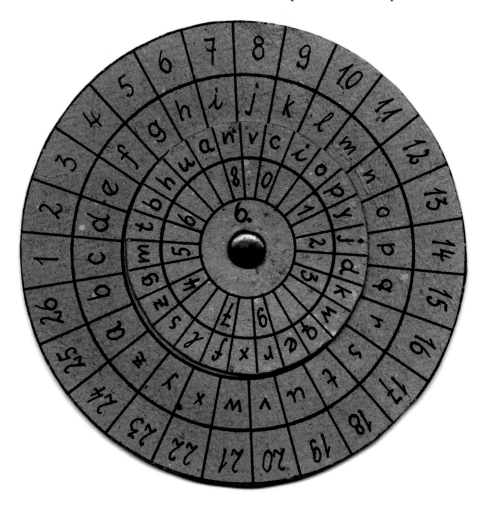

Code wheel found in the possession of the German spy Werner Walti (1941). *KV 2/1705*

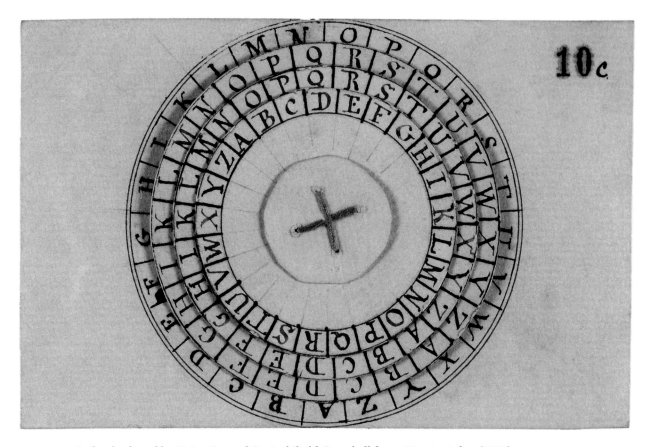

Code wheel used by Major General Sir Archibald Campbell for writing in cipher (1788). *PRO 30/11/202*

letter sent from Joseph Bonaparte, the recently installed King of Spain, to Napoleon that provided a full account of French operations and plans. The interception of French letters and dispatches to and from the battlefield, and the work of Scovell's codebreakers, played an important role in British victories at Oporto, Salamanca and Vitoria.

Following the Congress of Vienna in 1816, the work of the Secret Office was gradually scaled back due to the increasing sophistication of ciphers and the growing reticence expressed in some quarters that the government of the day should not possess the powers to intercept other people's letters. The citizens' right to privacy was contested in *The Times*, which argued that it was better for two dozen letters to be opened and read than for the nation to be shocked by some monstrous outrage. This viewpoint is as germane today as it was in the nineteenth century. The Secret Office was eventually closed in 1847 following public disquiet over the revelation that the Home Secretary had been secretly reading the mail of Giuseppe Mazzini, an Italian nationalist living in exile in London. Thus, at a time when Morse code and the electric

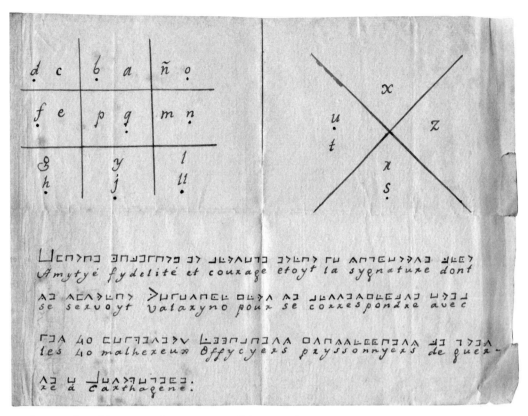

Cipher employed by General George Scovell (1808-14). *WO 37/12/9*

telegraph were beginning to replace mail as the primary means of communication, Britain deprived itself of one of its most useful sources of intelligence.

The outbreak of the First World War led to considerable advances in both the interception of enemy signals and the development of counter-measures to ensure secure and reliable communications. The Admiralty's Naval Intelligence Division and its communications section (NID 25), which was responsible for monitoring and deciphering Imperial German Navy signals, spearheaded British efforts. In October 1914, SMS *Magdeburg*, a German cruiser, ran aground on the island of Odensholm on the Estonian coast following an engagement with the Russian navy. The German crew destroyed the forward section of the ship but left behind three codebooks, together with the encryption key, one of which was delivered to the First Lord of the Admiralty Winston Churchill. The intelligence haul was later supplemented when a copy of the Verkehrsbuch (traffic book) was recovered from a sunken German destroyer. The information enabled the Royal Navy to track the movements of most German warships and mount successful ambushes.

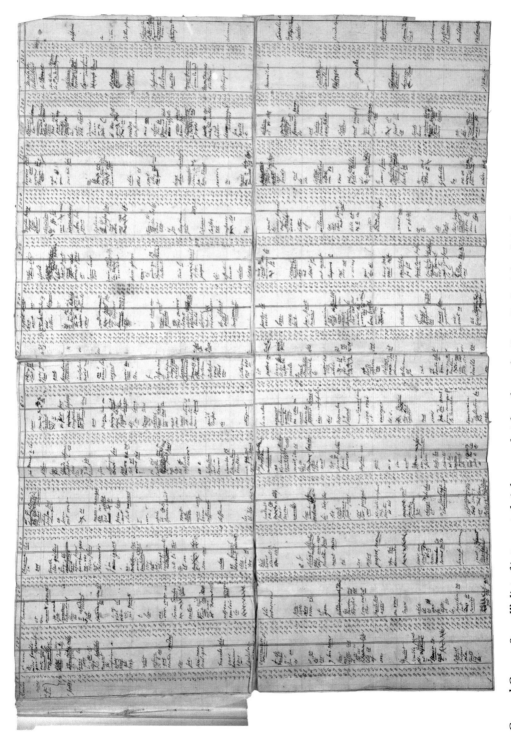

General George Scovell's list of interpreted cipher words taken from the Great Paris cipher (1812). *WO 37/9*

— 34 —

Dreisterne.

Lfde. Nr.	Sternsignal	Bedeutung
78	★★ ★★ / ★★ ≈	~~Ausführungszeichen [f. S. 29 u. Schießübungssignale S. 90] Hafenverteidigungssignal~~ [s. S. 82]
79	☆ ☆ ★	Erkennungssignal S. M. Schiffe bei Begegnungen mit deutschen Postdampfschiffen [s. S. 74]
80	☆ ☆ ★	
81	☆ ★ ★	[s. Aufklärungssignale S. 70] — Im Frieden, wenn Verwechselungen ausgeschlossen, außerdem für Übungszwecke verfügbar
82	☆ ★ ★	
83	☆ ★ ★	
84	★ ★ ★	
85	★ ★ ★	
86	★ ★ ★	
87	★ ★ ★	
88	1 Rakete	
89	2 Raketen gleichzeitig	
90	1 Rakete und ☆ ☆ ☆	
91	1 oder 2 Raketen und ☆ ☆ ★	
92	1 oder 2 Raketen und ★ ★ ☆	Aufklärungssignale
93	1 oder 2 Raketen und ☆ ★ ★	
94	1 oder 2 Raketen und ★ ★ ★	
95	1 oder 2 Raketen und ★ ★ ★	
96	1 oder 2 Raketen und ★ ★ ★	
97	1 oder 2 Raketen und ★ ★ ★	

Viersterne.

Lfde. Nr.	Sternsignal	Bedeutung
98	☆ ☆ ☆ ☆	
99	☆ ☆ ☆ ★	
100	☆ ☆ ☆ ★	
101	☆ ☆ ★ ★	
102	☆ ☆ ★ ★	
103	☆ ☆ ★ ★	
104	☆ ★ ★ ★	
105	★ ★ ★ ★	Sammelsignale für Torpedobootsflottillen.
106	★ ★ ★ ☆	Die Halbflottillen feuern unmittelbar nach dem Erlöschen des Viersterns noch ★ oder ★ [s. S. 104]
107	★ ★ ★ ★	
108	★ ★ ★ ★	
109	★ ★ ★ ★	
110	★ ★ ★ ☆	
111	★ ★ ★ ★	
112	★ ★ ☆ ★	

Three pages from the signal code book captured from the German cruiser *Magdeburg*.
ADM 137/4156 (18v), ADM 137/4156 (88) and ADM 137/4156 (20)

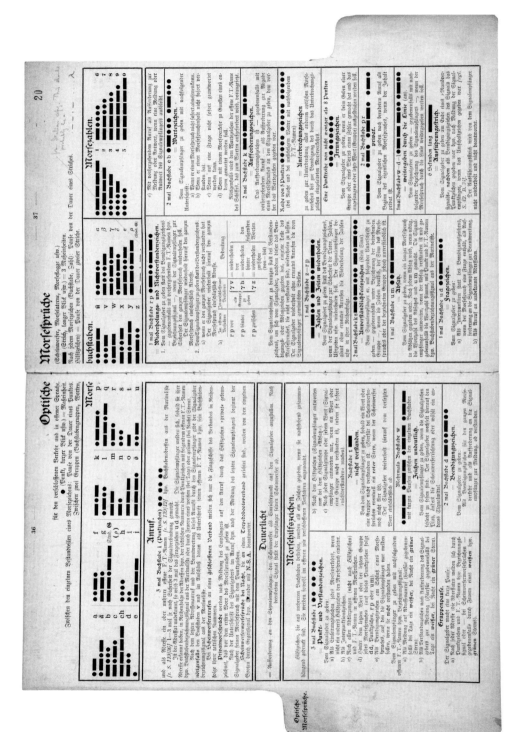

In recognition of their increasing importance, the naval codebreakers were re-housed closer to operational commanders in Room 40 of the Admiralty Building in Whitehall. One of the greatest achievements of Room 40 was to bring the United States into the First World War on the side of the Allies in the spring of 1917. The story begins in January when the German Foreign Minister, Arthur Zimmermann, transmitted a secret coded message to his ambassador in Washington, Count Johann von Bernstorff. The content of the message was dynamite. Bernstorff was informed that the German High Command had taken the decision to intensify the U-boat campaign in the western Atlantic and that unrestricted submarine warfare, including the sinking of neutral American shipping, would commence on 1 February. This policy broke previous undertakings given to US President Wilson concerning the safety of US vessels crossing the Atlantic. To further enflame American sentiment, the telegram proposed a military alliance between Germany and Mexico. In return for Mexican support in the event of the United States entering the war, Germany promised the return of Mexican territory in Texas, New Mexico and Arizona. Bernstorff was directed to transmit the message to Heinrich von Eckardt, the German ambassador to Mexico.

Germany's ability to communicate with its diplomats abroad was severely limited. At the outbreak of the war, a British naval vessel, *Teconia*, had cut the German international cables making the direct transmission of telegrams between Berlin and Washington impossible. To underline their neutrality both Sweden and the United States allowed limited use of their diplomatic cables for Germany to communicate with its ambassador in Washington. The transatlantic cables to America passed through a relay station at Porthcurno in Cornwall, where the signal received a boost prior to its long journey under the ocean. In utmost secrecy, British intelligence had managed to tap into the relay station at Porthcurno, enabling them to intercept all diplomatic traffic exchanged between Berlin and Washington. Zimmermann's encoded telegram to Bernstorff was duly intercepted and passed onto the Admiralty's codebreakers in Room 40.

The significance of the message was clear. The difficulty was how to inform Washington of its contents without revealing that the British were reading US diplomatic cables. Initially, Britain did nothing. The Director of Naval Intelligence, Reginald 'Blinker' Hall, believed that any disclosure would compromise Room 40's activities and resisted attempts to make the information public. Germany's resumption of 'unrestricted' U-boat attacks on British and neutral shipping made this position untenable. A plan soon began to emerge of how best to inform the Americans about the content of Zimmermann's telegram without disclosing the means by which it was obtained. It was known that the telegram would be forwarded from Washington to the German legation in Mexico City, using an older cipher that had already been broken by Room 40. If a copy of the encoded telegram could be obtained, this

GERMAN WIRELESS SIGNALS.

N.B. These vary from time to time

BP	I am ready to receive.
CHI	Cypher telegram of a tactical nature.
DD	Communication interrupted.
FA	Reply follows.
FF	The rest later.
FO	End of message.
FS	Message interfered with by jamming
KR	Urgent and important cypher telegram of a tactical nature.
MG	Increase of current [? Increase current]
MR	Motor troubles.
NF	There is no other station free [a reply to WR]
NV	Not understood.
OH	Transmit with a higher note.
OI	" " " lower note.
OS	Message finished. Ready to receive [? FO. BP]
US	Atmospherics interfering
YE	Understood.
WDH	Please repeat.
WG	Decrease of current [? Decrease current]
W?G	How are signals.
WR	Wait till I call.
XX	We are off [when the tactical situation necessitates the immediate dismantling of a station
ZIF	Cipher telegram of a technical nature.

Special Signals.

Begins	— · — · —	repeated	twice.
Stop [separation]	— · · · —	"	once
Wait	· — · · ·	"	twice *
Understand	· · · — · (VE)	"	twice
Rub out	· · · · · · · · · ·	about nine dots.

* Sometimes with indication of the number of minutes in the form WW15

Room 40 logbook containing German wireless signals. *ADM 223/767*

could then be deciphered and shared with the American authorities. In early February, one of Hall's agents was authorised to bribe an employee of the Mexican telegraph company to steal a copy of the message. On 24 February, Hall handed the decoded telegram to the US ambassador in London, Walter Hines Page.

The British cover story was that one of their agents in Mexico had obtained a copy of the deciphered telegram. In private, the British informed the Americans that they had broken the German code and demonstrated how this had been achieved. This allowed the United States' government to authenticate the message independently, using their own commercial telegraphic records stored in Washington. The Americans agreed to back the official cover story and the full text of the telegram was released to the Associated Press on 28 February 1917. Britain's ability to hoodwink both America and Germany as to the true source of the telegram had paid off handsomely. The United States remained unaware that its diplomatic traffic was being read by the British, and Germany embarked on a futile witch-hunt to track down a mythical traitor in its Mexican embassy. The story was a sensation and made headline news across the world. Those opposed to American involvement in the war claimed it was a British

Pen portrait of Reginald 'Blinker' Hall, Director of Naval Intelligence during the First World War. *HW 3/6 (4)*

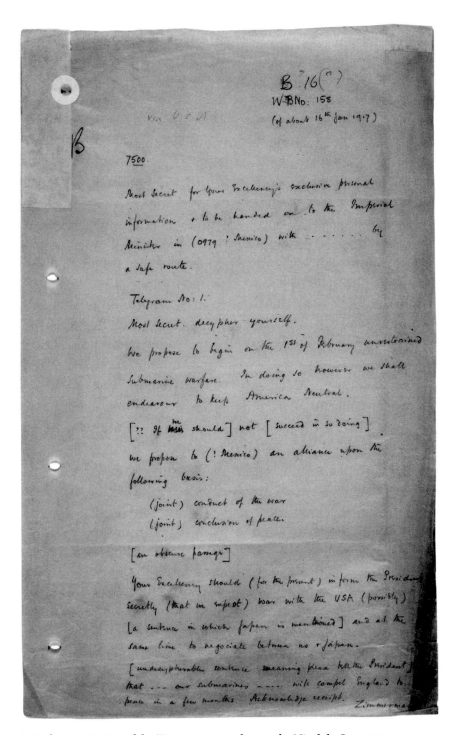

B 16 (?)
W.B.No: 158
(of about 16th Jan 1917)

Via U.S.A.

B

7500.

Most Secret for Your Excellency's exclusive personal information + to be handed on to the Imperial Minister in (0979 : Mexico) with . . . . by a safe route.

Telegram No: 1.

Most Secret. decypher yourself.

We propose to begin on the 1st of February unrestrained Submarine warfare. In doing so however we shall endeavour to keep America Neutral.

[?? If we should] not [succeed in so doing] .

we propose to (? Mexico) an alliance upon the following basis:

(joint) conduct of the war
(joint) conclusion of peace.

[an obscure passage]

Your Excellency should (for the present) inform the President secretly (that we expect) war with the USA (possibly) [a sentence in which Japan is mentioned] and at the same time to negociate between us + Japan.

[undecypherable sentence meaning please tell the President] that . . . our submarines . . . . will compel England to peace in a few months. Acknowledge receipt.
Zimmerman

Initial transcription of the Zimmermann telegram by Nigel de Grey. *HW 7/8*

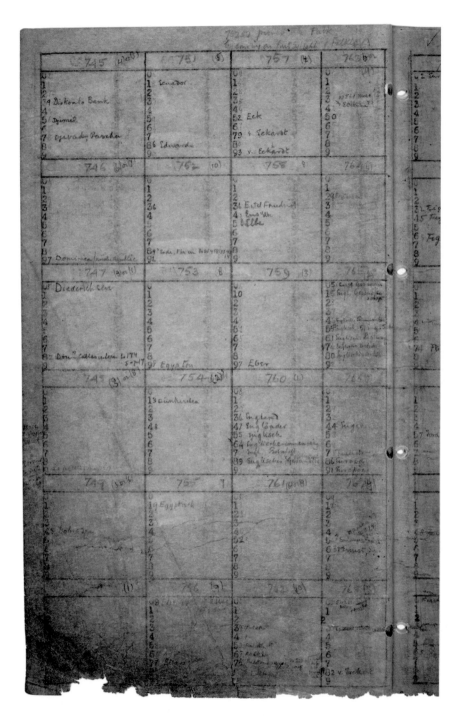

Two pages taken from the German code book 13040, used for encoding the Zimmermann telegram. *HW 3/176 (11v), HW 3/176*

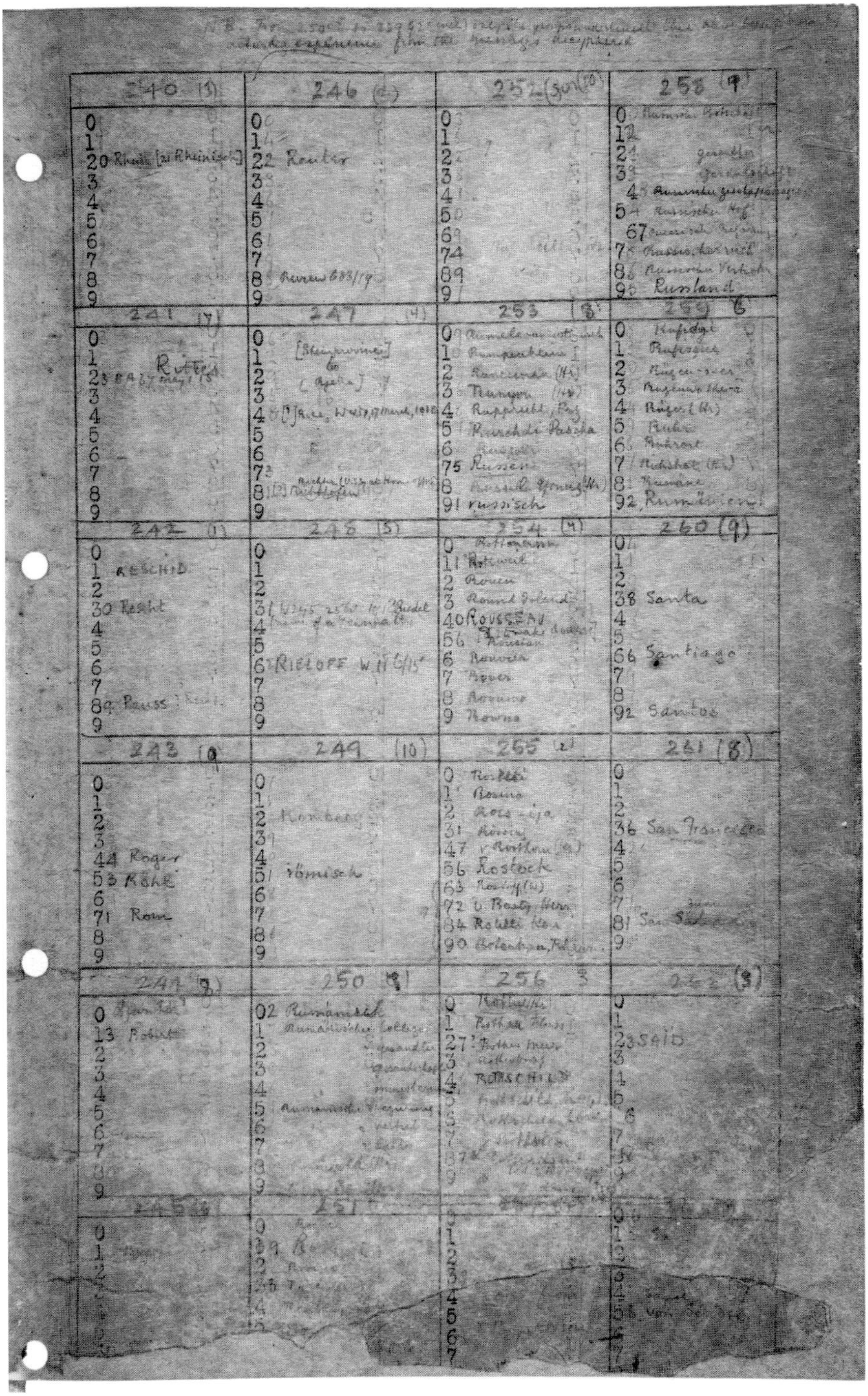

A photographic reproduction of a handwritten codebook page, largely faded and difficult to read. Partial transcription of legible entries by code-group number:

240 (3)
- 20 Rhein [zu Rheinisch]

246 (4)
- 14 22 Reuter
- Reuter 6 03/14

252 (30)(10)
- 74
- 89

258 (4)
- 12 Rumänien Botschaft
- 24 gesandte
- 34 Rumänische Regierung
- 5 Russische Hof
- 67 russische Regierung
- 7 Russ. kaiserl.
- 8 Rumänien Vertrieb
- 90 Russland

241 (7)
- Rutter

247 (4)
- [Bleyerwärmer] (?)

253 (8)
- Pumperheim
- 3 Tungen
- 4 Rapport, Bez
- Rüschdi Pascha
- 75 Russen
- 91 russisch

259
- 1 Professor
- 2 Ringen über
- 3 Rügen (H)
- 5 Ruhr
- 6 Ruhrort
- 7 Robschut (Er)
- 8 Rumäne
- 92 Rumänien

242 (1)
- RESCHID
- 30 Rescht
- 89 Rauss [Reuss]

248 (3)
- 3 (l 0345 25 01 to) Bidel
- 6 TRIELOFF W 11 6/15

254 (4)
- Rottomann
- 11 Rottwell
- 2 Rouen
- 3 Round Island
- 40 ROUSSEAU
- 56 Roussin
- 6 Rovigno
- 7 Rover
- 8 Rovino
- 9 Rovna

260 (9)
- 38 Santa
- 66 Santiago
- 92 Santos

243 (0)
- 44 Roger
- 53 Köhl
- 71 Rom

249 (10)
- Romberg
- romisch

255 (2)
- 0 Rorbeti
- 1 Romo
- 2 Rosa-eja
- 31 Rossi
- 47 Rosslau (a)
- 56 Rostock
- 63 Rossitz (4)
- 72 u Rosty Horn
- 84 Rosetti Herr
- 90 Rotenburg Köln

261 (8)
- 36 San Francisco
- 81 San Salvador

244 (3)
- 13 Robert

250 (5)
- 02 Rumänisch
- Rumänische Lotte
- gesandt
- gesandte
- Rumänische Regierung

256
- Rottula
- 1 Rottlub Herr
- 27 Rotan Herr
- Rothschild
- 4 ROTHSCHILD
- Rothschild Herr

262 (3)
- 23 5610

245
- Rogen

251
- 19 Rochel

Decrypted German diplomatic message carried on Swedish cable. *HW/7/8*

From Washington
To Mexico.

Feb. 19. 17.

(de Grey's decypher)

[Repetition of W No: 168 in 7500]

No 61

The Foreign Office telegraphs on Jan: 16. No: 1

Decypher yourself.

We intend to begin on the first of February unrestricted submarine warfare. We shall endeavour in spite of this to keep the USA neutral.

In the event of this not succeeding we make Mexico a proposal of alliance on the following basis:

Make war together
Make peace together

Generous financial support and an understanding on our part that Mexico is to reconquer the lost territory in Texas, New Mexico, & Arizona.

The settlement in detail is left to you.

You will inform the President of the above most secretly, as soon as the outbreak of war with the USA is certain and add the suggestion that he should on his own initiative invite Japan to immediate adherence + at the same time mediate between Japan + ourselves.

Please call the President's attention to the fact that the ruthless employment of our submarines now offers the prospect of compelling England in a few months to make peace.

Acknowledge receipt.

Zimmermann

Nigel de Grey's final decryption of the Zimmermann telegram. *HW 3/187*

SECRET.

L.W.   March 2nd 4 p.m. 1917.

Bell this morning took the cipher text of the
German message contained in your telegram of yesterday to the
Admiralty and there himself deciphered it from the German code
which is the Admiralty's possession.

The first group, 130, indicates Bernstorff's
number of telegram, number there. The second group, 13042,
indicates the code to be used in deciphering it.   From the
third group onwards the message reads:

"Auswaertiges Amt telegraphiert Januar 6. Nummer
ein ganz geheim selbst zu entziffern. Wir beabsichtigen am
ersten Februar uneingeschraenkt U-Boot Krieg zu beginnen.
Es wird versucht werden Vereinigte Staaten von Amerika
trotzem neutral zu erhalten. Für den fall dass dies nicht
genesingen sollte, schlagen wir Mexico auf folgend Grundlage
Bundnis vor. Gemeinsam Krieg führen. Friedenschluss.
Reichlich finanzielle Unterztutzung und ein Verstandnis
unserseits dass Mexico in Texas, Neu Mexico, Arizona früher
verlorenes Gebiet zürück eroberen. Reglung im einzelnen euch
Hochwohlgeborene überlassen. Sie wollen vorstehendes dem
Präsident streng geheim eröffnenm sobald Kriegsausbruch mit
Vereinigten Staaten fest steht und Anregung hinzufügen Japan
dem sich aus zu soehnen? ortige bei - ra - tung
einzuladen und gleichzeitig zwischen uns und Japan zu
vermitteln.   Bitte den Prasident darauf hinweisen, dass
rücksichtslos Anwendung unserer U-Boote jetzt Aussicht bietet
England in wenigen Monaten zum Frieden zu swingen.   Empfang
stätigen. Zimmermann. Schluss der Depesche".

Punctuations are given as in the German text. I
am sending decode into German group by group by tomorrow's
pouch.

Note explaining the deciphering of the Zimmermann telegram including text
in German. *HW 3/179*

Page's telegram to US Secretary of State.
(US Ambassador London.)

SECRET.

L.W.   February 24th 1 p.m. 1917.

Balfour has handed me the translation of a cipher
message from Zimmermann, the German Secretary of State for
Foreign Affairs, to the German Minister in Mexico, which was
sent via Washington and relayed by Bernstorff on January 19th.

You can probably obtain a copy of the text relayed
by Bernstorff from the cable office in Washington. The first
group is the number of the telegram, 130, and the second is
13042, indicating the number of the code used. The last but
two is 97556, which is Zimmermann's signature.

I shall send you by mail a copy of the cipher text
and of the decode into German, and meanwhile I give you the
English translation as follows:-

"We intend to begin on the 1st of February unrestricted submarine warfare. We shall endeavour in spite of this to
keep the United States neutral. In the event of this not
succeeding we make Mexico a proposal of alliance on the
following basis:-

'Make war together - Make peace together'. Generous
financial support and an understanding on our part that Mexico
is to reconquer the lost territory in Texas, New Mexico and
Arizona. The settlement in detail is left to you.

You will inform the President of the above most
secretly as soon as the outbreak of war with the United States
is certain and add the suggestion that he should on his own
initiative invite Japan to immediate adherence and at the same
time mediate between Japan and ourselves.

Please call the President's attention to the fact that
the ruthless employment of our submarines now offers the prospec

of

Copy of Walter Page's telegram to the US Secretary of State explaining the
background to the Zimmermann telegram. *HW 3/179*

hoax designed to stir up anti-German sentiment. Any further doubts as to the authenticity of the telegram were soon removed by Zimmermann himself who, in a speech in the Reichstag, admitted that the telegram was genuine. Zimmermann claimed that the alliance with Mexico was only intended to come into force if America attacked Germany and that its purpose was to maintain the neutrality of the United States. If this was the plan it was an abject failure. On 6 April 1917, the United States declared war on Germany. In his address to Congress, the US President, Woodrow Wilson, used the existence of the telegram as proof that Imperial Germany was now a direct threat to the peace and security of the American people.

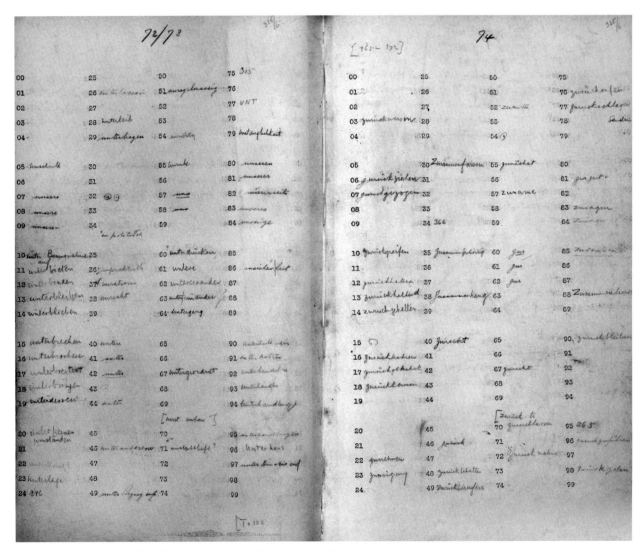

Two pages taken from a German code book used during 1916. *HW 3/176*

— 26 —

B.

Bagagen	447	Brennlänge	470
Bahn (Eisen-, Feld)	448	Brennzünder (Bz.)	471
Bataillon	449	Brieftaube	472
Batterie	450	Brigade	473
Befehl	451	Brücke	474
bei, beim	452	*[handwritten]*	475
beobachten, beobachtet	453	*[handwritten]*	476
Beobachter	454	*[handwritten]*	477
Beobachtung gut	455	*[handwritten]*	478
Beobachtung unmöglich	456	*[handwritten]*	479
Beobachtungsstelle	457	*[handwritten]*	480
Bereitschaft	458	*[handwritten]*	481
Bereitschaftstruppenkdeur (B.T.K.)	459	*[handwritten]*	482
		[handwritten]	483
beschädigt, beschädigen	460	*[handwritten]*	484
beschießen, beschießt	461	*[handwritten]*	485
		[handwritten]	486
besetzen, besetzt	462	*[handwritten]*	487
Bewegung	463	*[handwritten]*	488
Bindestrich	464		489
bis	465		
blau	466		
Blaupunkt	467		
Blindgänger	468		
Bogenschuß	469		

— 27 —

C.

chiffrieren, chiffriert	490	er, es	511
	491	erbeten, erbitten	512
		Erhöhung	513
D.		*[handwritten]*	514
Dauerfeuer	492	*[handwritten]*	515
Deckung	493	*[handwritten]*	516
dicht	494	*[handwritten]*	517
Division	495	*[handwritten]*	518
Drahthindernis	496	*[handwritten]*	519
dringend	497	*[handwritten]*	520
Drittel	498	*[handwritten]*	521
Dunst	499		
durch	500		
[handwritten]	501		
[handwritten]	502		
[handwritten]	503		
[handwritten]	504		
[handwritten]	505		
	506		

E.

eigen, eigene	507
einschießen, eingeschossen	508
Einzelfeuer	509
Entfernung	510

Example of a German army code book from the First World War. *ADM 137/4392 (26-27)*

CHAPTER 2

THE GOVERNMENT CODE AND CYPHER SCHOOL

After its success during the First World War, the Admiralty was anxious to consolidate its work in code breaking and ciphers. The Cabinet's Secret Service Committee, chaired by Lord Curzon, agreed and recommended that a peacetime code breaking agency should be created. The task of creating the new agency and coordinating its activities was given to the newly appointed director of naval intelligence, Commodore (later Admiral) Hugh Sinclair. The new agency was called the Government Code and Cypher School (GC&CS) and was formally established on 1 November 1919. It was soon installed in plush accommodation at Watergate House in the Strand, next to the Savoy Hotel in central London. The name was chosen deliberately to be unassuming and to deflect attention away from its clandestine activities. The acknowledged function of GC&CS was 'to advise as to the security of codes and cyphers used by all government departments and to assist their provision'. It was also given a secret directive 'to study the methods of cypher communications used by foreign powers'. This code breaking activity accounted for the majority of its resources. The first recruits to the new agency consisted staff from Room 40 and its army equivalent MI1b which dealt with War Office ciphers.

In comparison to other military units, GC&CS was relatively small, consisting of twenty-five intelligence officers and a similar number of clerical staff. Its operational head was Commander Alastair Denniston, founder of Room 40 and holder of an Olympic bronze medal won by the Scottish hockey team at the 1908 Games held in London. While the size of the new organization was modest, its remit was extensive. The primary objective given to Denniston and his team was to intercept and decipher diplomatic messages sent by foreign governments to their embassies and legations based in London. The interception of diplomatic traffic, in contrast to postal interception, required no warrant and was used extensively by British authorities. The legal basis for this activity was contained in the 1920 Official Secrets Act that provided the British government with the authority to obtain copies of any telegram transmitted on imperial territory within 10 days of transmission. By the 1920s, most of the international telegraph networks were either owned by British companies or passed through the territory of the British Empire. This outcome provided

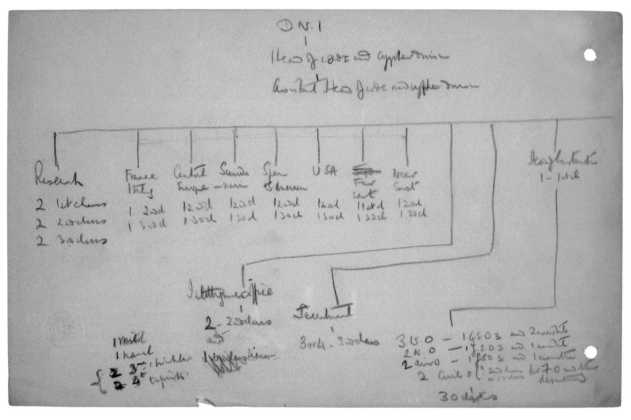

Handwritten note outlining the organisation of the Government Code and Cypher School (1919).
HW 3/34

GC&CS with unparalleled access to the bulk of diplomatic traffic. The countries targeted by GC&CS in this early period included France, Germany, Italy, Turkey and America.

The deciphered telegrams of foreign governments were regarded within Whitehall as the most valuable source of secret information respecting the policy and actions of foreign governments. They provided the most accurate and cheapest means of obtaining secret political information. To fully understand the significance of the messages required constant communication with staff at the Foreign Office. In 1922, to reflect its increased diplomatic role and to manage its activities more effectively, GC&CS was placed under the administrative and budgetary control of the Foreign Office. Its clandestine activities soon came to dominate its work and in 1923 it was placed under the operational control of the Secret Intelligence Service (SIS). Its newly appointed head, Hugh Sinclair, was given the title of Chief of the Secret Service and Director of GC&CS. The working relationship between the two organizations became even closer in 1926, when both were transferred to their new

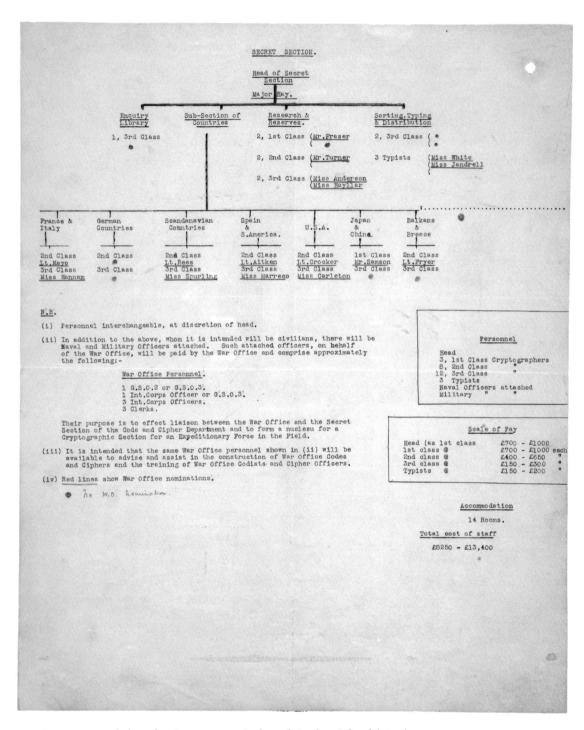

Organisational chart for Government Code and Cypher School (1919). *HW 3/34*

headquarters in Broadway Buildings, overlooking St James's Park tube station, with GC&CS occupying the third and fourth floors. In addition to its diplomatic activities, its military function was enhanced by the creation of dedicated service sections for the navy, army and air force that could be easily integrated into operational commands at the outbreak of war.

Throughout the 1920s and 1930s, one of the main targets for GC&CS was the Soviet Union and its attempts to foster revolution within the British Empire, the Middle East and central Asia. The Russian section of GC&CS was responsible for intercepting and deciphering traffic between Moscow and London. It was headed by Ernst Fetterlein, a

SECRECY

This may seem a simple matter. It should be. But repeated experience has proved that it is not. Even for the cleverest of us ; even for the least important. Month after month instances have occurred where [wor]kers at B.P. have been heard casually saying outside B.P. things that are dangerous.

It is not enough to know that you must not hint at these things outside. It must be uppermost in your mind every hour that you talk to outsiders. Even the most trivial-seeming things matter. The enemy does not get his intelligence by great scoops, but from a whisper here, a tiny detail there. Therefore:—

DO NOT TALK AT MEALS. There are the waitresses and others who may not be in the know regarding your own particular work.

DO NOT TALK IN THE TRANSPORT. There are the drivers who should not be in the know.

DO NOT TALK TRAVELLING. Indiscretions have been overheard on Bletchley platform. They do not grow less serious further off.

DO NOT TALK IN YOUR BILLET. Why expect your hosts who are not pledged to secrecy to be more discreet than you, who are?

DO NOT TALK BY YOUR OWN FIRESIDE, whether here or on leave. If you are indiscreet and tell your own folks, they may see no reason why they should not do likewise. They are not in a position to know the consequences and have received no guidance. Moreover, if one day invasion came, as it perfectly well may, Nazi brutality might stop at nothing to wring from those that you care for, secrets that you would give anything, then, to have saved them from knowing. Their only safety will lie in utter ignorance of your work.

BE CAREFUL EVEN IN YOUR HUT. Cleaners and maintenance staff have ears, and are human.

There is nothing to be gained by chatter but the satisfaction of idle vanity, or idle curiosity: there is everything to be lost—the very existence of our work [and] the lives of others, even the War itself.

[Pe]ople will always be curious. They can always learn something from your answers, *if* you answer, even though you only answer 'Yes' or 'No'. Do not suggest, as is so easy, and so flattering to human vanity, that you are doing something very important and very 'hush-hush'. Far too many people in England know that about Bletchley Park already. If ever the Germans come to know it, we may find ourselves a German 'Target for To-night'. There are drawbacks to publicity.

The only way, then, is to cut the conversation short. For example:—

Question. What are you doing now ?
Answer. Working for the Foreign Office (or other Ministry as appropriate).
Question. But what do you *do* ?
Answer. Oh—work.

A gay reticence in that vein will win you far more real respect from anyone worth respecting, than idle indiscretion or self-important airs of mystery.

There is an English proverb none the worse for being seven centuries old:—

Wicked tongue breaketh bone,
Though the tongue itself hath none.

I hereby promise that no word of mine shall betray, however slightly, the great trust placed in me.

Signed

O.U.P. Form No. 18.

Personal security form signed by all staff working at the Government Code and Cypher School. *HW 14/36*

former cryptographer in the court of Tsar Nicholas II, who had fled Russia following the Bolsheviks seizure of power in 1917. On his arrival in England, he was recruited by Room 40, where he was given the task of breaking Georgian, Austrian and Bolshevik codes. In the aftermath of the revolution, the new Soviet government abandoned the Tsarist codes it had inherited, believing them to be fatally compromised. To protect their diplomatic communications, the Soviets resorted to low level manual ciphers which proved relatively easy to break. For the British government, the most valuable intercepts were the diplomatic telegrams sent from Georgy Chicherin, the Soviet Foreign Minister to the Soviet Trade Delegation in London, which at the time was the only official Soviet presence in Britain. The intercepted messages provided the government with invaluable insights into the negotiating position adopted by the Soviets in their attempts to re-establish Anglo-Soviet trade and to restore diplomatic ties between the two countries.

Further successes occurred in July 1920, when GC&CS intercepted a series of radio messages between Chicherin and the deputy commissar for foreign affairs, Maxim Litvinov. The messages concerned the activities of the *Daily Herald*, a national newspaper with a circulation of 300,000 that championed socialist causes and supported militancy among the British trade union movement. The intercepted cables revealed Moscow's financial support for the newspaper, including smuggling parcels of cash and jewellery into the country using the diplomatic cover provided by the Soviet Trade Delegation. On receiving the information, the Cabinet's initial response was to expel the entire Russian delegation. On reflection, the complete disruption of diplomatic ties between the two countries was considered a step too far. It was also felt that the ability of the intelligence agencies to monitor Soviet actions would be lost if the entire delegation was ordered to leave the country. Instead, the government took the surprising decision to make the intercepts public by releasing them to sympathetic newspapers. On 19 August, *The Times* printed the story under the headline 'The Daily Herald…Orders from Moscow', including printed exchanges of telegrams between Chicherin, Litvinov and Leonid Krasin, the leader of the Soviet Trade Delegation. The story detailed the various payments handed over to the *Daily Herald* by the Soviets in return for advancing Bolshevist ideology and endorsing its leading role in directing civil unrest and upholding workers' rights. The publication of the story caused panic at the offices of the *Daily Herald*, with the director of the paper, Francis Meynell, making plans to flee the country, fearing arrest on charges of treason and sedition. Moscow either failed to notice the story or did not appreciate its full significance, and took no immediate action to change its ciphers. To avoid interception, the Soviets were forced to rely on trusted couriers to deliver diplomatic messages. New ciphers were eventually introduced by the Soviets, but these were soon broken by Fetterlein and the Russian section of GC&CS.

Mr. Longhurst.

[This Document is the Property of His Britannic Majesty's Government.] **320**

Printed for the Cabinet. December 1920.

CONFIDENTIAL

THE RUSSIAN TRADE AGREEMENT.

NOTE BY THE SECRETARY OF STATE FOR FOREIGN AFFAIRS.

IN the discussions about the above agreement, I have throughout confined myself to urging that the political assurances given by the Soviet Government—and described by us in our note of the 20th June as "the fundamental condition of any trading agreement"—should neither be evaded nor whittled away, nor should evaporate in misty generalities, leading to indefinite procrastination and barren disputes. I was afraid that unless we were very much on the alert the Russians might get their Trade Agreement, while we should lose what is, in my view, our sole *quid pro quo*, viz., the cessation of Soviet hostilities and propaganda, both at home and in the East. From the abundant evidence at our disposal, it looks as though my fears were in danger of being realised even more quickly than I had imagined.

At the Cabinet of the 20th November I pointed out—from the testimony of their own utterances—that the Soviet leaders did not mean their political assurances, in so far as they were referred to or repeated in the Trade Agreement, to have any immediate or binding application. They were to be made the subject of a future political conference, attended by political delegates from Russia and Great Britain, and this conference was to develop into the Peace Conference, which is their real aim, and to carry with it the recognition of the Soviet Government by Great Britain.

When I asked the Cabinet whether, assuming this to be the Soviet policy, it was one which we were prepared to accept, I was assured that nothing of the kind was in contemplation; that references to the areas to which the Soviet assurances of desistance from propaganda or hostilities were intended more particularly to apply would be inserted in the preamble, and that the meaning which His Majesty's Government attached to them would further be elucidated in a letter to be handed to M. Krassin at the same time as the agreement was signed.

We now know that the exact procedure which I ventured to anticipate has been followed. In repeated telegrams between Chicherin and Krassin the former has laid down, and the latter has acted upon, the contention that our preamble, containing the afore-named references, must be rejected; that all references to particular spheres of political activity must be expunged; that the commercial clauses "*are immediately to come into action*, while the political preliminaries are *merely the groundwork in principle for ensuing political negotiations*." (Chicherin to Krassin, the 3rd December, 1920.)

The most outspoken of these revelations is probably that contained in another message of the 5th December from Chicherin to Krassin :—

"We refuse to add even a single letter to the July agreement. *Without a political conference we cannot limit our activity in the East,* since only at such a conference will the concrete obligations that bind us be compensated by concrete obligations binding England. *Without this we refuse to bind ourselves.*"

In other words, the political assurances which the Soviet Government accepted as long ago as July are to be worth nothing until they have been explored and certified by a political conference at a later date; at this conference each item of the indictment is to be disputed and met by counter-charges, and nothing is to be conceded unless it is balanced by some corresponding assurance on the part of Great Britain. Such a conference may well last for months, and in the interval (while the Russians are enjoying the, to them, immeasurable advantages of British trade) the propaganda and the hostilities will pursue their career unchecked.

That this is the aim of the Soviets is further demonstrated by their alarm at the provisions in the preamble that in case of conspicuous violation of the terms of the

378 [5115]

The Russian Trade Agreement, 1920. *CAB 24/116/86*

2

agreement by either party, it may forthwith be denounced by the other, and by the pressure which they are applying to get the minimum period of notice extended to six months.

I once again plead with my colleagues not to allow ourselves to be cheated by these tactics. There are two alternatives before us. One is to adhere to the preamble which was approved on the 26th November (although some of us would have greatly preferred that it should be made stronger and more specific). The other is to yield to the Soviet plea that the political assurances can only be defined at a subsequent political conference summoned *ad hoc*—in other words, they will remain in abeyance until we succeed in coming to an agreement with the Bolsheviks as to their exact meaning and application.

If we adopt the latter policy, it seems to me that we shall have abandoned the greater part of what we have been fighting for, and that we shall be left with only the remotest chance of mitigating or stopping Bolshevik hostilities and propaganda at all.

On the former occasion I pleaded that the fulfilment of the political conditions should be anterior to the conclusion of the Trade Agreement. The Cabinet decided that it should be simultaneous. It is now proposed that it should be indefinitely subsequent. I hope that this stratagem may be defeated, and that our preamble will be retained.

C. OF K.

December 13, 1920.

In May 1927, British police and Special Branch officers raided the offices of the All Russian Cooperative Society (ARCOS) searching for Top Secret documents. The impetus behind the raid came from a tip off from a former employee of ARCOS who informed the security services that classified material including a War Office training manual had been smuggled into its offices in Moorgate which it shared with the Soviet Trade Delegation. It was widely believed that ARCOS was little more than a commercial front to conceal its real activities of espionage and subversion. During the raid, which lasted several days, the police found numerous classified documents stored in the basement and a secret cipher room in which officials were hurriedly burning papers. This and other intelligence convinced the authorities that ARCOS was a front for Soviet espionage. The immediate success of the raid, however, was more than outweighed by the intelligence disaster that followed in its wake. The Soviets were incensed by the raid. They believed it represented a flagrant breech of the 1921 trade agreement that granted diplomatic immunity to both ARCOS and the Soviet Trade Delegation. The British government countered by accusing Moscow of using ARCOS to conduct military espionage and subversive activities.

The raid placed the British government in a dilemma. Criticized by its own back benches for allowing Soviet subversion to proceed unchecked, the government decided to sever diplomatic relations with Moscow and expel the trade delegation. To justify its actions, the government took the decision to publish a number of incriminating documents. The material made public not only included documents obtained from the raid, but messages intercepted by GC&CS that confirmed Soviet espionage. In contrast to the revelations of 1920, the Russians immediately recognized the source of the documents and abandoned their diplomatic ciphers in favour of one-time pads that were virtually impossible to break. The top sheet of the pad was designed to be torn off and destroyed after use. To increase security, sheets of highly flammable nitrocellulose were often used that could be quickly burned after use. The episode meant that GC&CS could no longer decipher Soviet diplomatic traffic and deprived Britain of an important source of intelligence, with little to show in return.

In the absence of diplomatic traffic, GC&CS increasingly directed its efforts to breaking Soviet military ciphers. In the early 1930s, naval and military intercept stations began to detect an increase in traffic exchanged between Moscow and a number of clandestine radio stations. It was soon discovered that the messages were from the Comintern, an international communist organization that advocated world revolution and which directed the work of national communist parties. The task of identifying and decoding the messages was led by Lieutenant Colonel John Tiltman, a mathematician and former cryptanalyst with the Indian Army responsible for decoding Russian cipher traffic in Afghanistan and central Asia. The operation was codenamed

'Mask' and began to locate the various radio stations that were active in Britain. One of these stations was located in a residential house in Wimbledon, South West London, which was occupied by a known member of the Communist Party with connections to William Morrison, a radio operator. Over the next few years, Tiltman was able to break the Comintern cipher. The messages were enciphered with use of an encoded alphabet derived from a book held by both correspondents. This was usually a dictionary, but a telephone directory and books of poetry were sometimes used. Operation Mask produced a wealth of information which was shared with the Security Service (MI5). The messages revealed that the Soviets were actively developing a network of saboteurs inside British dockyards with the intention of preventing armed aggression against Russia in a future war. The Mask decrypts revealed the identities of Soviet agents and provided details of financial contributions to various communist front organizations. The details were passed to the Security Service with the ringleaders in the dockyards dismissed from their jobs.

By the mid-1930s, Nazi Germany began to replace Soviet Russia as the main target for GC&CS. In May 1938, a German section was established. This followed the German annexation of Austria in March when 100,000 German troops took over Austria in a matter of days. The occupation came as a surprise to Britain and its allies and demonstrated that Germany could mobilise its armed forces without any noticeable clues being detected from intercepted communications. To encode their messages, the Germans relied on the use of the Enigma machine. Initially designed in the 1920s for use in banks and businesses that required secure communications, the Enigma machine resembled a portable typewriter with each letter connected to an illuminated display board via a system of electromechanical rotors. To add further complexity, the rotors were connected to a plug board on the front of the machine where pairs of letters were transposed. When a key was depressed, a small bulb would illuminate a letter in the display panel. There was no consistent pattern to the process making it virtually impossible to break the code. Enigma was operated by a two-man team: one to generate the letters and the other to send the enciphered message in Morse code via a radio transmitter. To decode the message at the other end, the operator needed to know the configuration of the rotors and cables on the first machine. The operator would then type out the coded message which would appear in plain text on the illuminated panel. The arrangement of the rotors and cables were reset on a regular basis further increasing the security of the message. The Enigma machine was soon adopted by the German military, with the navy taking possession of its first machine in 1926. By the early-1930s, the Germans were using Enigma to encode both their diplomatic and military communications.

Alexander Ilitch BIRKENGOFF

Alexander Ilitch Birkengoff has, since his arrival here on 21.9.26., as Assistant Manager of the Chemical Department of Arcos been the subject of three anonymous letters. The allegations against him in these letters may be summarised as follows:

1. He is a dangerous Russian spy.

2. He is the first authority on all matters of Bolshevik propaganda in this country.

3. Before his arrival in England he worked for the G.P.U. as a District Commissar.

4. He has no business qualifications.

It is further alleged by an individual, who is believed to be the writer of the anonymous letters referred to above, that Birkengoff receives £100 monthly from Russia, £60 for himself and £40 for propaganda purposes, that he often goes to the London Docks to meet Russians arriving or departing, and that both he and his son are ardent Communists and extremely anti-British. Verification of certain particulars in the anonymous letters show that they are correct in so far as the movements of the various individuals are concerned. Confirmation of the allegations made in 1, 2 and 3 above has also been obtained from other reliable sources.

(a) It has been definitely ascertained that Birkengoff is a full member of the V.K.P.(b), as is also Joseph Litvine-Gurevich, with whom he resides at 22, Highfield Avenue.

(b) A reliable informant has stated that when Ethel Chiles alias Kathe Gussfeldt visited this country in 1927, she was to get into touch with Vassili Vassilievitch BARABANOV of the Arcos Steamship Company, under whose orders she was to work. When proceedings against Ethel Chiles developed and there were signs that her identity might become known, Barabanov decided to leave this country. (In confirmation of this it may be noted that

MI5 Report on Alexander Illitch Birkengoff, Director of Arcos. *KV 2/2488*

51A

- 2 -

indications regarding the identity of Ethel Chiles may have
reached the Russians about the time of Barabanov's application
for a Return Visa to Russia and back on 27.4.27.   It is also
worth noting that he never availed himself of the return half
of his visa).

P.F.R. 4130 BOROCH.

        In the employ of Barabanov was a certain [Kousma KHAZAINOV,]
who had also previously been engaged in espionage activities, as
a result of which the Russians thought that it would be better if
they severed all connection with him or got him out of the
country.   [Kousma KHAZAINOV,] had a daughter [Akolena,] who was a
typist in the Chemical Department of Arcos, and employed under
Alexander Birkengov.   At the time of the Arcos raid she left
some document lying about, which it is assumed related either to
political or espionage matters.   She was consequently warned to
get out of the country as quickly as possible, Birkengov paying
her the sum of £20 for her journey.   (In confirmation it may be
stated that Kousma Khazainov's personal file, which was examined
at the time of the Arcos raid, showed that this man had been
employed as a stoker at Arcos and that he had been dismissed
from Arcos in September, 1926. Peter Miller appears to have
interceded on his behalf, as a result of which he was seen by
Jilinsky and an arrangement was made for him to return to Russia.
The file also showed that Khazainov had been an exile in Siberia
in the Czarist days and that he was a full member of the V.K.P.(b).
With regard to his daughter, records show that she did in fact
leave the country voluntarily about a fortnight after the Arcos
raid).   Information has also been received from one who is well
placed to know that Akolina Khazainova was connected in a minor
capacity with the Macartney case.   There is therefore some colour
to the suggestion put forward in the anonymous letters that
Birkengov is engaged in espionage matters, and in the opinion of a
reliable informant it is at least probable that Barabanov's duties
in this connection were taken over after his departure by
Birkengov.

- 3 -

(c) Information has also been received that <u>Birkengov</u> served for a considerable period in the Red Army and that after that he worked for the G.P.U. in Russia until he was sent abroad. As regards his services in the Russian Army it is stated on his Registration Card that he served from 1912-21. The statement regarding his work for the G.P.U. confirms the anonymous allegation

(d) Once in February and once in April, 1928, Birkengov paid a visit to Glasgow, but the nature of his activities there are not known. On his return, however, he held a conference with KONEVETZ and LITVINE-GUREVICH, both of whom are known to be extremely undesirable from a political point of view.

(e) Definite information was obtained before the Arcos raid showing that Birkengov was taking an interest in factory and working conditions in this country and in Germany.

(f) As evidence of Birkengov's political standing, it is interesting to note that when Leah PODOLSKY of the inner circle of Arcos and a joint member of the Russian and British Communist Parties, travelled to Germany in April last, she carried credentials signed by Birkengov to a prominent member of the Berlin Trade Delegation.

COPIED TO: F1A12.

Copy behind — New pd.n.
ST 413/5   368

William MORRISON.

Address: No.761376 Civilian Wireless Reserve,
           215 Earlsfield Road,
           Wandsworth, S.W.18.

MORRISON has had his instructions that in the
event of a general mobilisation he is to report immediately
to the Personnel Transit Centre at R.A.F. Station, Farnborough.

The above named member of the Civilian Wireless
Reserve is known to be in possession of certain information
which M.I.5 and S.I.S. are particularly anxious to have. The
facts of the case are, very briefly, as follows:-

1.   From 1934 onwards, S.I.S. and M.I.5 were aware
that there was constant illicit wireless transmission
between London and Moscow. The station here was located
in January 1935 and from that time M.I.5 were able to
obtain every message that was transmitted from the Comintern
to this country and the replies. By this means were
found out the exact amounts of the subsidies to various
subversive organisations here - the Communist Party of
course and the "Daily Worker" - the identity of Soviet
couriers and the policy pursued by the Comintern in
connection with the general election here, the civil war
in Spain and other political events.

2.   During the period January 1935 to October 1937
there were three different locations for the illegal
transmission centre, and a number of changes in the
technical personnel. By careful watching we were able to
establish the identity of the personnel and the very few
members of the Communist Party here who were allowed to
deal with them.

3.   William MORRISON was the operator of the
transmitting stations at Wimbledon, Buckhurst Hill and
Hersham, from April 1935 until October 1937, since which

MI5 Mask Report on William Morrison. *KV 2/606*

-2-

date we have been unable to pick up any messages at all
to this country.

4.   At the beginning of October 1937, MORRISON left
the Hersham address, the wireless mast was taken down and
the house left empty.   On the 23rd October 1937 he went
to Spain to fight in the International Brigade.   On the
23rd April 1938 he returned from Spain, and I have a very
shrewd suspicion that he deserted.   After his arrival he
and his wife went to live in rooms.   For some considerable
time MORRISON never left the house and made absolutely no
attempt to get into touch with any of his communist friends.
This may have been because he was no longer interested in
communism, or because he did not wish the separation
allowance which his wife was drawing to be cut off.

5.   For a very long time MORRISON was out of work
and extremely hard up, his wife was working as a waitress,
and I am pretty confident that MORRISON had no connection
at all with the Communist Party.   In June of this year
it was found that MORRISON was working with a firm - Peto-
Scott Limited - as a tester of wireless sets for the Air
Ministry.

6.   It has also been ascertained that shortly after
joining the firm MORRISON enrolled in the Civilian Wireless
Reserve.

          Having obtained a great deal of information in
regard to MORRISON over a long period, I am pretty confident
that, although strongly anti-fascist, he is not primarily a
man interested in politics.   I think he is the adventurous
type who will take on anything which will give him fresh
experience and interest.   He started life in the Navy and
deserted in Alabama in 1926.   He was then wireless operator
in a Swedish ship for several years.

          It would be of the greatest value to M.I.5 if

-5-

MORRISON could be interviewed with a view to obtaining as much information as possible under the following headings:-

Full details of the organisation of the illicit transmission of messages between Moscow and London, including -

a) The date it was started.

b) The reason why the three stations we know of were closed down.

c) The reasons given to MORRISON for his dismissal.

d) Any knowledge he has of the present method of secret communication between the Comintern and this country.

e) The present activities of the remainder of the personnel of the illicit wireless stations.

f) All the information of which he is in possession as regards the illegal underground organisation of the Communist Party here.

Unknown to the Germans, the Polish Cipher Bureau had managed to obtain a commercial version of the Enigma machine and by 1933 had devised a method enabling them to read German radio messages enciphered using Enigma. The Poles used this information to build several replicas of the Enigma machine similar to those used by the German navy and air force. Fearing invasion, the Poles decided to share their knowledge with Britain and France. In January 1939, the first meeting of the countries' code breakers took place in Paris. Participants included the head of GC&CS, Alastair Denniston, his French counterpart, Captain Gustave Bertrand, and the head of the Polish Cipher Bureau, Lieutenant Colonel Karol Gwido Langer. A further meeting took place in the Kabaty Woods south of Warsaw in July, where the Poles finally revealed how they had cracked the German codes and handed over a replica of the Enigma machine to the British. The machine was secretly spirited from the country and on 16 August, two weeks before the outbreak of the Second World War, it was presented to Stewart Menzies, then deputy head of SIS.

Early photograph of an Enigma typing machine.

Patent for lifting mechanism for lifting out drums of the Small Enigma
N° 267,472.

PATENT SPECIFICATION

Convention Date (Germany): March 25, 1924.

231,502

Application Date (in United Kingdom): March 25, 1925. No. 8027/25.

Complete Accepted: Oct. 29, 1925.

COMPLETE SPECIFICATION.

Improvements in Ciphering Machines having a Plurality of Ciphering Rollers for Effecting Substitution of the Signs.

We, CHIFFRIERMASCHINEN AKTIEN-GESELLSCHAFT, of Steglitzerstr. 2, Berlin, W. 35, Germany, a German company, do hereby declare the nature of this inven-
5 tion and in what manner the same is to be performed, to be particularly described and ascertained in and by the following statement:—

Ciphering machines (for example elec-
10 trical ciphering machines) are already known wherein a plurality of ciphering rollers are arranged, which have on their end faces a number of contacts by means of which they touch one another. These
15 rotatable ciphering rollers are arranged between fixed end drums. The contacts at one end of the ciphering rollers are connected with the contacts at the other end through the ciphering rollers in the
20 most irregular manner possible and the contacts of one fixed end drum are con-nected with actuating points, for example key contacts, while the contacts of the other fixed end drum are connected with
25 indicating devices, for example glow lamps, or with a writing mechanism.

In consequence of this arrangement the electric current, upon the actuating point being struck, for example upon the
30 key of the letter c being depressed, passes in an irregular manner through the system of the ciphering rollers (compare Figure 1) and yields, for example at the indicating points, the letter h.
35 Now the method is also known of rotat-ing the ciphering rollers relatively to one another during the ciphering of a rather large number of single signs, so that the system of sign substitution is altered,
40 that is, so that at the next depression of the letter key c, the letter m, for example, appears at the indicating points.

It is further to be observed that the contact points on the ciphering rollers
45 are provided in such numbers as corre-

spond to the signs to be substituted, for example twenty-six contacts correspond-ing to the twenty-six letters of the alphabet.

In the case of such an arrangement the 50 ciphering rollers, after a comparatively small number of ciphering operations return to their initial position so that in the case of the example selected the letter c again gives the code sign h, that is to 55 say, the period of the ciphering recom-mences. The shorter the period of the ciphering is, the easier it is for an unauthorised person to decipher a coded message. 60

Now according to the invention an arrangement is provided which yields an exceedingly long period, so that decipher-ing by unauthorised persons by observing repeating substitutions is practically 65 impossible.

Thus, care is taken to adjust the cipher-ing rollers easily into a definite position relatively to one another, to make this position clearly intelligible, and to 70 return the ciphering rollers quickly to any desired initial position.

The invention is illustrated by way of example in the accompanying drawings wherein: 75

Figure 1 is a perspective view of four ciphering rollers with their contact points and driving mechanisms (for the better elucidation of the course of the current the ciphering rollers are shown somewhat 80 separated from one another).

Figure 2 is a view of the ciphering rollers with part of the driving and adjusting mechanism, partly in section.

In Figure 1 for the sake of clearness 85 only six contact points are shown, while in Figure 2 a larger number are indi-cated, corresponding to the practical con-struction of the machine.

In the case of the constructional 90

[Price 1/-]

British patent specification submitted for the Enigma ciphering machine, 1925.

Four photographs of the Enigma machine, one showing plug board and connectors.

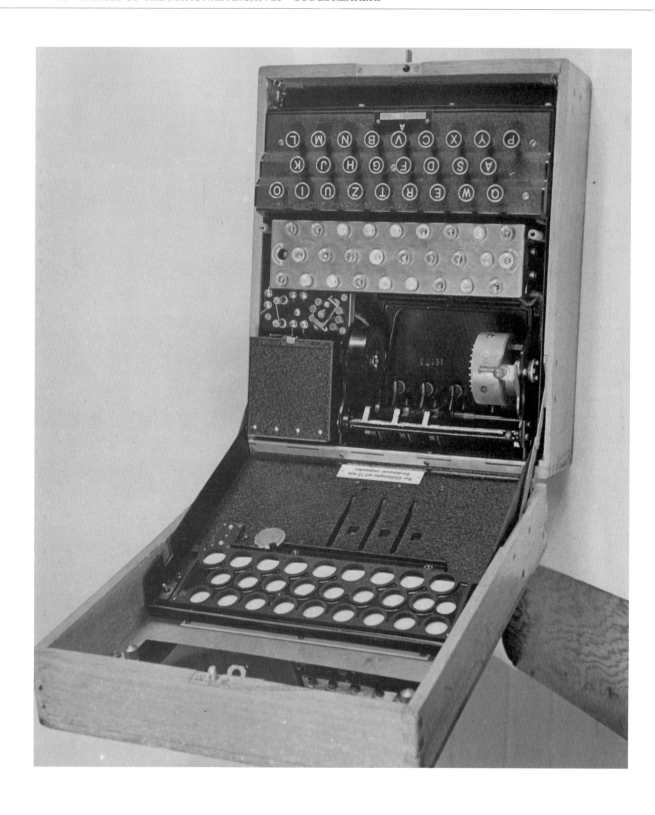

CHAPTER 3

ULTRA GOES TO WAR

Located in Broadway Buildings in central London, GC&CS was expected to be a major target in the event of war with Nazi Germany. In August 1939, a month before the outbreak of war, the entire GC&CS staff were relocated to Bletchley Park, a large country estate in Buckinghamshire far away from potential enemy bombing. In an attempt to disguise its function, the organization was renamed the Government Communications Headquarters (GCHQ) and was known variously as Station X, Room 47 Foreign Office and BP. At the beginning of the war, staff numbers at GC&CS were about 150, but this figure soon grew dramatically. The wartime recruits at Bletchley Park were primarily selected for their knowledge of mathematics and linguistics but they also included a

Propaganda postcard showing Winston Churchill overseeing battle plans. *CN 11/6/12*

mix of chess players and crossword enthusiasts. Initially, GCHQ followed the pre-war recruitment policy, and sought recruits through contacts at Oxford and Cambridge universities. These included Alan Turing, the mathematician and cryptanalyst who invented the world's first programmable computer, Bill Tutte who broke the German Lorenz cipher and Gordon Welchman who specialised in traffic analysis of encrypted German communications.

As the codebreaking process became more automated and the volume of intercepted communications grew, many more staff were recruited from a wider range of backgrounds. A significant proportion of these came from the Women's Services including the WAAF, the WRNS and the ATS with the remainder recruited through the Civil Service. These included Jane Fawcett, who decoded the message leading to the sinking of the German battleship *Bismarck*; Tommy Flowers, the designer of Colossus, the world's first electronic computer; and Jim Rose, the future literary editor of the *Observer* and chairman of Penguin Books. Family ties were also important. Nigel de Grey and Dillwyn Knox, both veterans of Room 40, recruited their sons, and Evelyn Sinclair, the sister of Hugh Sinclair, the former chief of SIS, joined the staff at Bletchley in the summer of 1940. To accommodate the new recruits, prefabricated wooden buildings were erected in the courtyard of Bletchley Park. These soon became known as 'Huts' with each focusing on specific subject areas. Foremost amongst these were Huts 3 and 6, where Enigma messages transmitted by the German army and air force were decrypted, translated and analysed for vital intelligence; Huts 4 and 8 which were responsible for breaking and analysing naval Enigma; and Hut 11 which housed the main computing section. The interception of German transmissions was a vital aspect of Bletchley Park's work. This was provided by listening stations located at Beaumanor Hall, Leicestershire, Beeston Hill in Norfolk and Chicksands in Bedfordshire. Once intercepted, the coded messages were written down on paper by hand and sent to Bletchley by motorcycle dispatch riders for decryption and analysis.

In the early stages of the war, German codes delivered to Bletchley Park were broken using pen, paper and brainpower. The codebreakers working without the benefit of electro-mechanical devices sifted through hundreds of enciphered letters. The first breakthrough came in October 1939, when the Luftwaffe Enigma key was partially broken. This insight indicated that air force operations in support of Operation Sealion, the Nazi invasion of Britain planned for September 1940, had been postponed. The Blitzkrieg offensive conducted by the German armed forces required the close coordination of air force and army units. This gave some clues into the army's operational orders, but it was not until 1943 that the Wehrmacht Enigma codes were fully understood and broken.

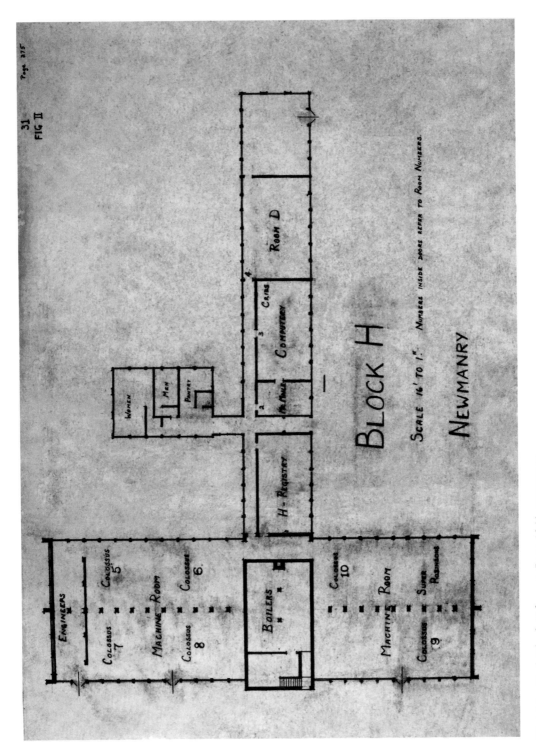

Bletchley Park Block H layout, June 1941. *HW 25/5 (2)*

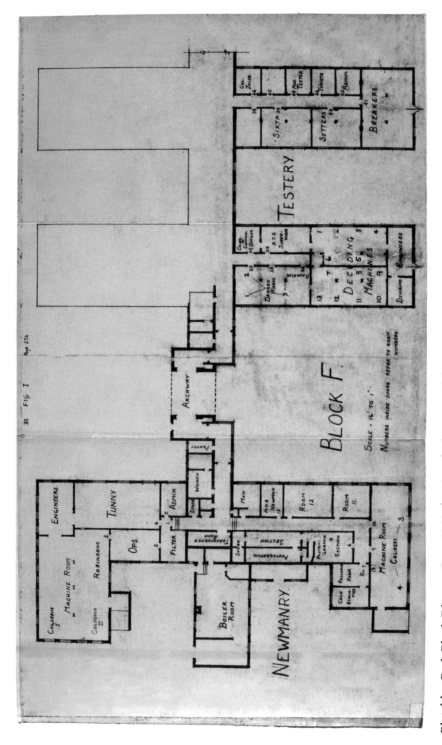

Bletchley Park Block F layout, June 1941 showing the location of the Newmanry and Testery. *HW 25/5 (1)*

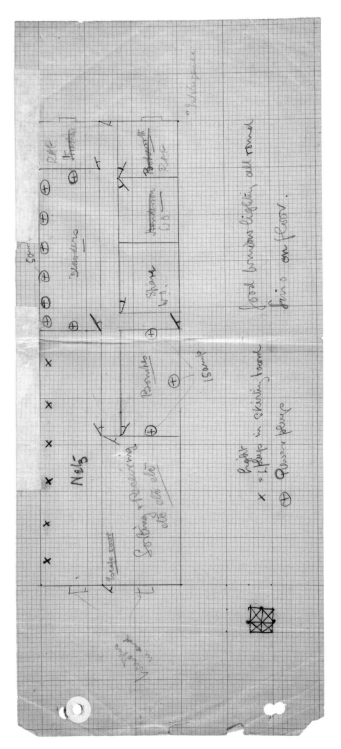

Hand drawn plan of the proposed hut layout for Bombe operations. *HW 14/1*

The German naval Enigma proved an equally difficult challenge to the codebreakers. This was partly due to the increase in available rotors – eight as opposed to five used by the army – and because the naval operators of the Enigma were more disciplined and made fewer errors, thus providing less compromised material for Bletchley Park to exploit. As British shipping became more vulnerable to German U-boat attack, the need to break the German naval codes became an urgent necessity. The key to eventual success was provided by a series of daring raids designed to capture Enigma machines and code books. The first raid took place in March 1941, when British commandos raided the Lofoten Islands off the coast of Norway and seized a set of Enigma rotor wheels and its code book from the German armed trawler *Krebs*. This was followed by further operations against two weather-reporting trawlers the *Munchen* and its sister ship the *Lauenburg* that yielded important cipher material. The most important operation took place in May 1941 with the capture of the German U-boat *U-110* which was forced to surface following attack from HMS *Bulldog*. The submarine's captain was unable to scuttle the boat and a boarding party was sent on board to discover an intact Enigma machine, a code book and ciphering keys. The captured material was sent to Bletchley Park and within days, Hut 8 was reading a constant flow of traffic transmitted by the German navy.

Operation Claymore: British special forces raid on the Lofoten Islands off the coast of Norway showing oil tankers ablaze, 4 March 1943.

Operation Claymore: British commandos watching as fish oil tanks are set on fire, 4 March 1943.

Bletchley's success did not go unnoticed. The Prime Minister, Winston Churchill, received daily transcripts of Ultra material delivered personally to Downing Street by Desmond Morton, his personal assistant on intelligence matters. In September 1941, Churchill visited Bletchley and gave a morale-boosting speech to staff. In spite of Churchill's visit, conditions at Bletchley began to deteriorate rapidly. It was under-resourced, badly managed and the victim of inter-service rivalry. The secret nature of Bletchley's work also meant that it could not use the normal channels to justify its ever-increasing demands. To break the log-jam, a number of the most influential staff at Bletchley, including Alan Turing and Gordon Welchman, wrote directly to Churchill pleading for more resources. On receiving the letter, Churchill was infuriated and demanded that GC&CS be given all the help it required. To ensure that this episode was not repeated, he ordered his military assistant Hastings 'Pug' Ismay to ensure resources were found and to report back on progress. Given the Prime Minister's personal support, the working conditions at Bletchley improved dramatically.

The success of British code breakers was due in part to the development of the world's first programmable digital computer known as Colossus that had been installed at Bletchley in 1943. Prior to the war, Alan Turing had developed the concept of a

Secret and Confidential.

Prime Minister only.

Hut 6 & Hut 8,
Room 47,
Foreign Office,
London, S.W.1.

21st. October 1941.   (Bletchley Park).

Dear Prime Minister,

Some weeks ago you paid us the honour of a visit, and we believe that you regard our work as important. You will have seen that, thanks largely to the energy and foresight of Commander Travis, we have been well supplied with the "bombes" for the breaking of the German Enigma codes. We think, however, that you ought to know that this work is being held up, and in some cases is not being done at all, principally because we cannot get sufficient staff to deal with it. Our reason for writing to you direct is that for months we have done everything that we possibly can through the normal channels, and that we despair of any early improvement without your intervention. No doubt in the long run these particular requirements will be met, but meanwhile still more precious months will have been wasted, and as our needs are continually expanding we see little hope of ever being adequately staffed.

We realise that there is a tremendous demand for labour of all kinds and that its allocation is a matter of priorities. The trouble to our mind is that as we are a very small section with numerically trivial requirements it is very difficult to bring home to the authorities finally responsible either the importance of what is done here or the urgent necessity of deal--ing promptly with our requests. At the same time we find it hard to believe that it is really impossible to produce quickly the additional staff that we need, even if this meant interfering with the normal machinery of allocations.

We do not wish to burden you with a detailed list of our difficulties, but the following are the bottlenecks which are causing us the most acute anxiety.

Letter sent to Churchill signed by Alan Turing, Gordon Welchman, Hugh Alexander and Stuart Milner-Barry requesting more staff and resources for Bletchley Park. *HW 1/155*

II

Breaking of Naval Enigma (Hut 8).

Owing to shortage of staff and the overworking of his present team the Hollerith section here under Mr. Freeborn has had to stop working night shifts.   The effect of this is that the finding of the naval keys is being delayed at least twelve hours every day.   In order to enable him to start night shifts again Freeborn needs immediately about twenty more untrained Grade III women clerks.   To put himself in a really adequate position to deal with any likely demands he will want a good many more.

A further serious danger now threatening us is that some of the skilled male staff, both with the British Tabulating Company at Letchworth and in Freeborn's section here, who have so far been exempt from military service, are now liable to be called up.

2.   Military and Air Force Enigma (Hut 6).

We are intercepting quite a substantial proportion of wireless traffic in the Middle East which cannot be picked up by our intercepting stations here.   This contains among other things a good deal of new "Light Blue" intelligence.   Owing to shortage of trained typists, however, and the fatigue of our present decoding staff, we cannot get all this traffic decoded. This has been the state of affairs since May.   Yet all that we need to put matters right is about twenty trained typists.

3.   Bombe testing, Hut 6 and Hut 8.

In July we were promised that the testing of the "stories" produced by the bombes would be taken over by the W.R.N.S. in the bombe hut and that sufficient W.R.N.S. would be provided for this purpose.   It is now late in October and nothing has been done.   We do not wish to stress this so strongly as the two preceding points, because it has not actually delayed us in delivering the goods.   It has, however, meant that staff in Huts 6 and 8 who are needed for other jobs have had to do the

III

testing themselves.   We cannot help feeling that with a Service
matter of this kind it should have been possible to detail a
body of W.R.N.S. for this purpose, if sufficiently urgent in-
-structions had been sent to the right quarters.

4.   Apart altogether from staff matters, there are a number of
other directions in which it seems to us that we have met with
unnecessary impediments.   It would take too long to set these
out in full, and we realise that some of the matters involved
are controversial.   The cumulative effect, however, has been
to drive us to the conviction that the importance of the work
is not being impressed with sufficient force upon those outside
authorities with whom we have to deal.

We have written this letter entirely on our own initiative.
We do not know who or what is responsible for our difficulties,
and most emphatically we do not want to be taken as criticising
Commander Travis, who has all along done his utmost to help us
in every possible way.   But if we are to do our job as well as
it could and should be done it is absolutely vital that our
wants, small as they are, should be promptly attended to.   We
have felt that we should be failing in our duty if we did not
draw your attention to the facts and to the effects which they
are having and must continue to have on our work, unless
immediate action is taken.

We are, Sir, Your obedient servants,

A. M. Turing
W. G. Welchman.
C.H.O'D. Alexander
P.S. Milner-Barry.

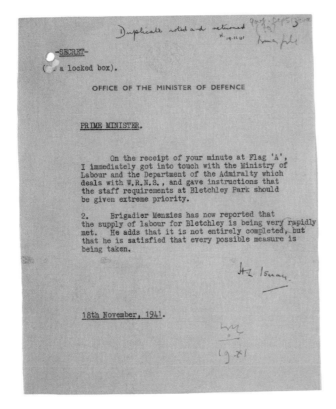

A note from Churchill demanding that Bletchley Park should get all it needs and a response from Hastings Ismay that staff numbers at Bletchley are increasing. *HW 1/155 (5), HW 1/155 (4)*

computing machine that operated using a predefined set of rules to determine a result from a set of variable inputs. Max Newman, the renowned mathematician, who arrived at Bletchley Park in August 1942, realized that such a machine would allow ciphers to be broken far more quickly than using manual methods. The work of the codebreakers was also supported by the installation of bombes, a type of rudimentary computer that worked out the daily settings of the rotors and plug boards on the Enigma machines used by the German military. The first bombe, code named Victory, was installed in March 1940 and by the end of the war over 200 of the machines had been housed in Bletchley and the surrounding area. Colossus computers were first used to help decipher intercepted radio teleprinter messages that had been encoded using the Lorenz cipher used exclusively by the German high command. Unlike Enigma, the Lorenz machine used a non-Morse method of transmission based on a Vernon stream cipher. All teleprinter messages were given the code name 'Fish' and those that were enciphered using the Lorenz machine were known as 'Tunny'.

Photograph of captured Lorenz cipher machine. *HW 25/4*

A series of photographs depicting Colossus and Tunny machines. *HW 25/26*

Photograph of a Colossus computer. *HW 25/26*

Back view of a Colossus computer showing the Thyratron rings. *HW 25/25*

Back view of a Colossus computer. *HW 25/25*

Side view of a Colossus 7 computer. *HW 25/25*

Photograph of Colossus 10. *HW 25/25*

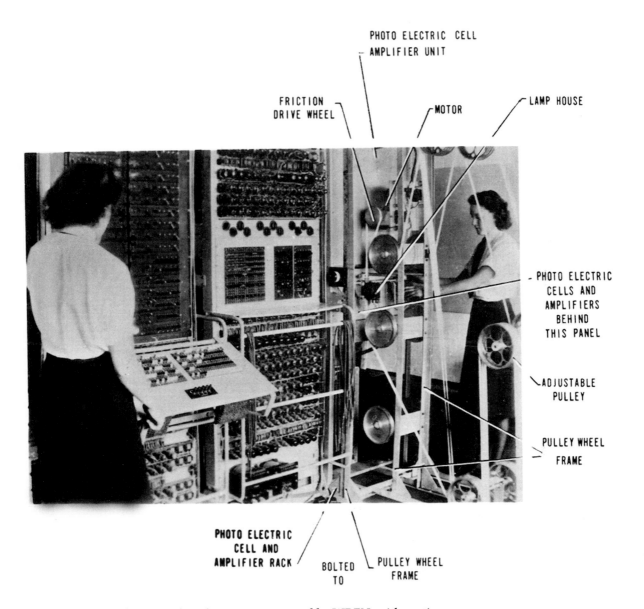

PHOTO ELECTRIC CELL
AMPLIFIER UNIT

FRICTION
DRIVE WHEEL

MOTOR

LAMP HOUSE

PHOTO ELECTRIC
CELLS AND
AMPLIFIERS
BEHIND
THIS PANEL

ADJUSTABLE
PULLEY

PULLEY WHEEL
FRAME

PHOTO ELECTRIC
CELL AND
AMPLIFIER RACK

BOLTED
TO

PULLEY WHEEL
FRAME

Colossus electronic digital computer operated by WRENs with captions. *FO 850/234*

Colossus electronic digital computer. *FO 850-234*

Front view of Colossus computer. *HW 25/26*

Photograph of Tunny machine on bench. *HW 25/26*

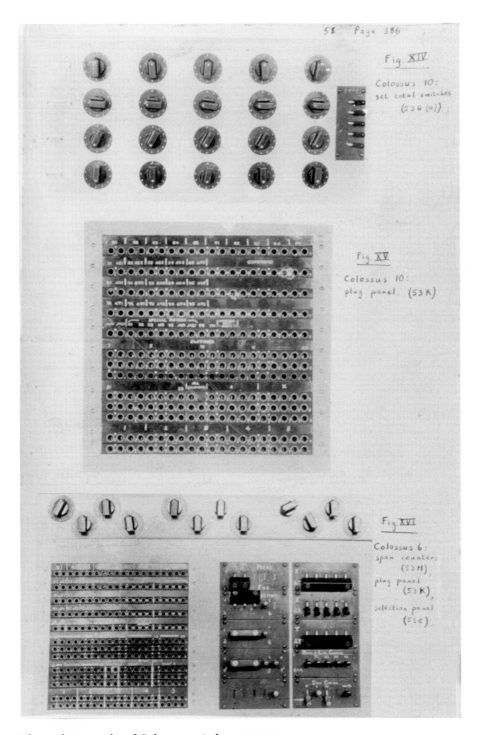

Three photographs of Colossus switches. *HW 25/2*

Photograph of a Proteus computer. *HW 25/5*

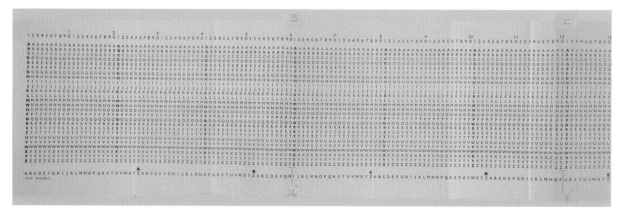

Allied codebreaking Banbury sheet. *HW 40/264*

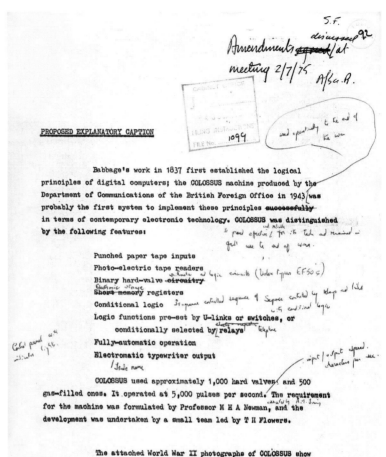

Proposed explanatory caption to accompany a photograph of Colossus released in 1975.

The volume of material handled by Bletchley Park increased dramatically as the war progressed and in 1942, GCHQ was split into two sections. The diplomatic and commercial sections were transferred to London and operated from 7-9 Berkeley Street, with Denniston as Deputy Director (Civil), while the military sections remained at Bletchley Park under Commander Edward 'Jumbo' Travis, Deputy Director (Services).

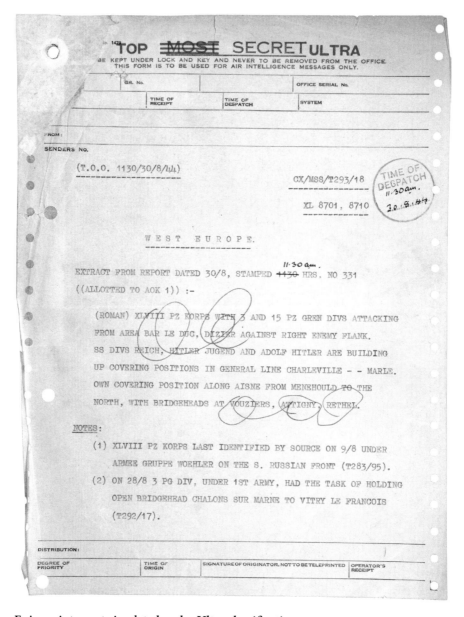

Enigma intercept circulated under Ultra classification. *HW 1/3196 (3)*

The interception of radio communications was not the sole preserve of GCHQ. In September 1939, the Radio Security Service (RSS) was established. Its role was to detect and locate illicit wireless communications made by German spies within Britain and its coastal waters. Initially under the control of MI8 of the War Office, and using physical facilities provided by the Post Office and a network of voluntary interceptors, RSS supplied the Security Service with details of intercepted communications. Headed by Colonel J.P.G. Worlledge, who had commanded the No. 2 Wireless Company in Palestine, RSS operated from headquarters at Arkley in north London. In December 1939, it intercepted a series of transmissions emanating from a German ship in the North Sea. The ship belonged to the Abwehr, the German intelligence service, and was being used as a mobile communications platform directing operations in Norway. The transmissions were of two distinct types: communications between the Abwehr and its overseas stations, which were encoded using Enigma; and messages to and from individual agents, which were encoded by hand using a book cipher.

The key to breaking the Abwehr codes was provided by a double agent, known as 'Snow'. A Welsh-born, naturalised Canadian and electrical engineer, Snow had volunteered to report information obtained during business trips to Hamburg to British intelligence. In September 1936, a letter from him to a known Abwehr correspondence address indicated

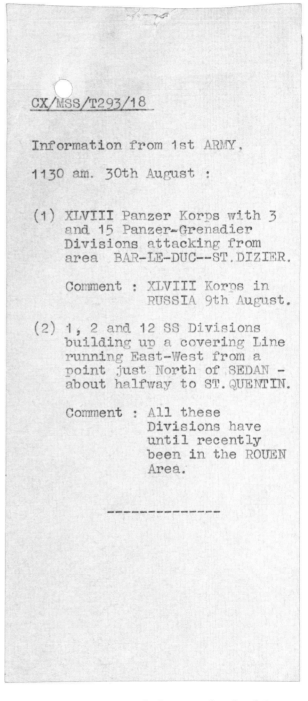

Enigma intercept giving deployment details of German 1st Army, 30 August 1944. *HW 1/3196 (2)*

that he was also reporting to the Abwehr. Confronted with the evidence, Snow admitted that he had been recruited by the Germans and following interrogation at Wandsworth prison, he agreed to resume communications with the Abwehr but under the direction of MI5. Unaware that Snow had been turned, the Abwehr provided him with a copy of its cipher to enable him to relay messages back to Germany. The cipher was immediately passed to Bletchley who were soon able to read all of the Abwehr's traffic transmitted by radio. The unit responsible for reading the hand ciphers was headed by Oliver Strachey – brother of the writer Lytton Strachey – and was given the code name ISOS (Intelligence Service Oliver Strachey). The Morse-encoded messages were decoded by Dillwyn Knox and in similar fashion were given the code name ISK.

The success of the RSS in reading the traffic of the Abwehr soon came to the attention of SIS, who were concerned that the Security Service was encroaching on the work undertaken at Bletchley Park. Menzies was adamant that all signals intelligence should be centralised and placed under the control of GCHQ, which ultimately reported to Menzies himself. The Prime Minister agreed and in May 1941, RSS was placed under the operation control of SIS with Lieutenant Colonel Ted Maltby replacing Worlledge as the organization's new head. RSS was given the designation Special Communication Unit (SCU) 3 and reported to SIS's Section VIII with facilities at Hanslope Park, near Milton Keynes, and Whaddon Hall, near Bletchley. The new arrangements allowed Abwehr traffic to be monitored on a constant basis. The volume and quality of the intercepted material enabled Bletchley to achieve one of its great triumphs. In December 1941, Dilly Knox decoded the Abwehr's Enigma cipher, providing valuable insight into German intelligence operations.

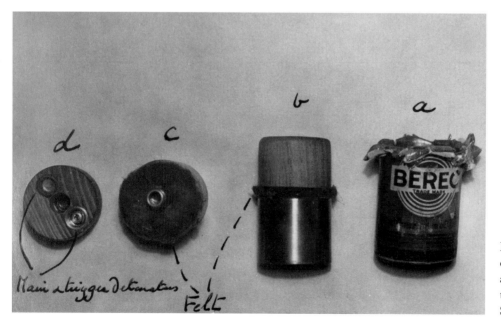

Detonators disguised as batteries used by agent Snow. *KV 2/450*

Secrecy was vital to the work of Bletchley Park. All staff were required to sign the Official Secrets Act with many refusing to discuss their work long after the true role of Bletchley Park had been made public. To maintain security, interception, decryption and analysis was carried out by separate sections. Only then was it sent out to the intelligence chiefs in the relevant ministries, and later on to high-level commanders in the field. To further disguise the fact that Britain was reading German communications, the intelligence derived from Bletchley Park was provided to the Services under the pretence that it had been acquired from a secret agent operating at the highest levels within the German military establishment. To provide further credibility for the story, the fictitious spy was given the code name Boniface. The system has its drawbacks, as the reports were often ignored as unreliable or misleading given the poor performance of SIS during the early stages of the

10, Downing Street,
Whitehall.

MOST SECRET.

September 27, 1940.

Dear C,

    In confirmation of my telephone message, I have been personally directed by the Prime Minister to inform you that he wishes you to send him daily all the ENIGMA messages.

    These are to be sent in a locked box with a clear notice stuck to it "THIS BOX IS ONLY TO BE OPENED BY THE PRIME MINISTER IN PERSON".

    After seeing the messages he will return them to you.

Yours ever,

P.S. As there will be no check possible here,
        would you please institute a check on receipt
C.   of returned documents to see that you have
        got them all back.

A note from Desmond Morton informing Stewart Menzies, the Chief of MI6, that Churchill wishes to be sent Enigma messages on a daily basis. *HW 1/1*

war. In June 1941, the hapless Boniface was retired from service and from that date forward all Enigma based signals intelligence was given the classification 'Ultra' – above Top Secret. To underline its importance, a daily digest of Ultra material was delivered personally to Winston Churchill. The intelligence in the digest was selected by Menzies and comprised summaries of the most important military and diplomatic decrypts, the so called 'golden eggs'. The daily summaries were delivered personally to the Prime Minister by Desmond Morton, his trusted intelligence adviser, in a locked briefcase to which Churchill and Menzies had the only keys. The golden eggs were eagerly devoured by Churchill, whose estimation of Menzies and the work of the secret service increased considerably.

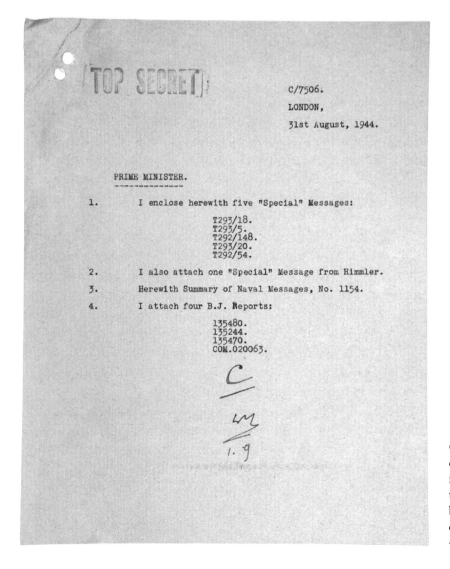

Cover sheet of Enigma intercepts sent to Churchill by the Chief of MI6.
HW 1/3196 (1)

CHAPTER 4

THE BATTLE OF THE ATLANTIC

The Battle of the Atlantic was the most prolonged and expansive military campaign of the Second World War. Beginning on the first day of the war in September 1939 and lasting until the defeat of Nazi Germany in May 1945, the conflict covered over 32 million square miles of ocean and stretched from the tip of South America to the Arctic Circle. The outcome of the battle was of crucial importance to both sides and helped to determine the outcome of the war. Surrounded by sea, Britain was heavily dependent on a constant flow of goods and supplies to feed its population and to carry on the fight against Nazi Germany. To knock Britain out of the war, Germany realized that it would first need to sink the supply convoys crossing the Atlantic before they could reach port and unload their valuable cargoes of food, fuel and military supplies. The Battle of the Atlantic was fought above and below the waves. The U-boats and battleships of the German Navy were locked in a deadly struggle against the Royal Navy as it sought to protect Allied shipping from attack. The defeat of the U-boat threat was central to British war aims and essential to the eventual defeat of Nazi Germany. If the U-boats gained the upper hand, Britain's outlook would be bleak. Faced with serious shortages of food and lacking oil and spare parts to re-equip its armed forces, the nation's ability to continue the war would be placed in serious doubt.

To issue orders and communicate over the vast distances of the Atlantic Ocean, both sides made extensive use of radio traffic to connect operational commanders to individual warships and submarines. To protect communications from enemy interception, the German navy relied on a version of the Enigma machine that was more complex than that of the other military services. To increase security, the naval Enigma had eight rotors, of which three were selected for each daily setting. Notches were also added to the alphabet ring that caused the rotors to jump one space when it reached a designated point on the ring. Further protection was provided by the codebooks and tables used by the Enigma's operator. These were printed in water-soluble red ink on pink paper. In the event of the submarine sinking or being captured, the pages would become unreadable when immersed in water. Given its complexity, the German Enigma naval codes proved difficult to break. To successfully decipher naval communications, the codebreakers at Bletchley desperately needed information that could only be supplied by the capture of German codebooks and other documents.

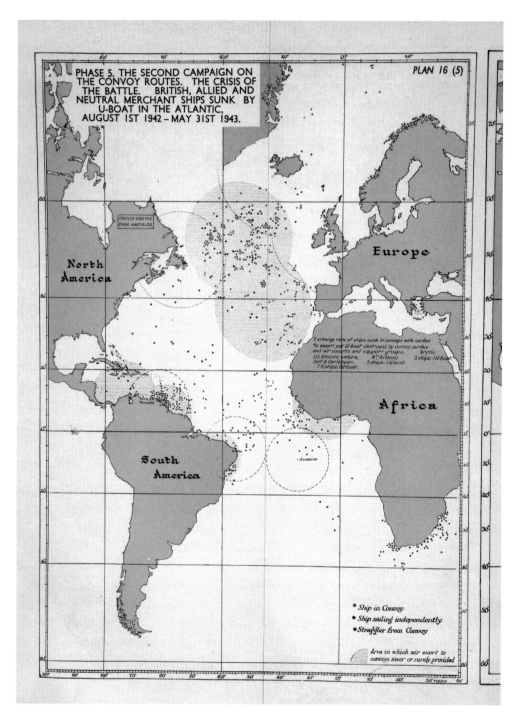

Map showing the number of Allied and neutral merchant ships sunk by U-Boats during **1942-43.** *ADM 234/579 No. 16 (5)*

The first step forward in breaking naval Enigma took place in January 1940. The episode began with the sighting of a German submarine laying mines in the Firth of Clyde off the west coast of Scotland. The submarine was the *U-33*, a 600-ton U-boat with a crew of forty which had previously attacked and sunk several trawlers off the coast of Ireland. The Admiralty immediately ordered HMS *Gleaner*, a Halcyon class minesweeper equipped with the latest underwater detection equipment, to the last known location of the *U-33*. The *Gleaner's* captain, Lieutenant Commander Hugh Price, soon located the submarine and dropped ten depth charges into the surrounding area. Seriously damaged by the explosions, the *U-33* was brought to the surface and the crew ordered to abandoned ship. The submarine was then scuttled by the captain and began to sink below the waves. Unfortunately, for the Germans, it came to rest in shallow waters just 40 metres below the surface. Royal Navy divers were dispatched to locate the wreck and recover anything of interest. The divers soon came across three intact Enigma rotors which were promptly delivered to Bletchley Park. The crew were interrogated and revealed that the German navy used four separate cipher keys that were transmitted as part of the message preamble. The four different keys depended on whether the message was intended for home waters, foreign waters, fleet messages or officers only, the latter being used for high level communications. To distinguish between them, codebreakers at Bletchley gave each key a codename: henceforth they would be known as Dolphin, Pike, Barracuda and Oyster respectively.

To fully decipher Dolphin and the other Enigma keys, Bletchley Park needed to reconstruct the codebook used to encipher the original message. As was shown earlier, this was successfully achieved in a series of audacious raids that resulted in the capture of an intact Enigma machine and number of codebooks. By the middle of 1941, Bletchley was able to decipher a steady stream of naval traffic. By reading the messages exchanged between Berlin and submarine commanders, the Admiralty's Operational Intelligence Centre was able to re-route the convoys to avoid U-boat patrol areas. The volume of Allied shipping lost to enemy attack dropped dramatically from 320,000 tons in June 1941 to an average of 91,000 tons in July and August. The intercepted messages also allowed the Admiralty to track the position of German surface raiders and mount successful counter-attacks. In November, the German cruiser *Atlantis* was intercepted and sunk by HMS *Devonshire* whilst rendezvousing with the submarine *U-126* at a location north of Ascension Island in the South Atlantic. Two days later the U-boat supply tender *Python,* which had arrived to refuel *U-126* and pick up survivors, was disabled and eventually scuttled following engagement with HMS *Dorsetshire.*

The success of British counter-measures and the continued failure of U-boats to locate convoys led elements in the German High Command to speculate whether the British had broken the naval Enigma. The head of the German U-boat fleet, Rear Admiral Dönitz, discounted the idea believing that espionage, luck or the use of high level radar were more

The British Cruiser HMS *Devonshire* firing its 8-inch guns. *CN 11/6 (19)*

likely explanations. Despite his contention that breaking Enigma was mathematically impossible, Dönitz ordered his U-boat fleet to use a special Enigma machine, the Triton M4, which was equipped with an extra rotor that could be set to any one of twenty-six possible positions. The addition of the fourth rotor meant that the messages produced by the Triton were unreadable by the codebreakers at Bletchley. The new machine was given the code name 'Shark' and following its introduction in February 1942, Bletchley was left in the dark as to the location of the German wolf packs.

The consequences were dreadful. Unable to re-route convoys to safe areas, the submarines could attack at will. In the first six months of 1942, only three U-boats were located and sunk. In contrast, throughout the whole of 1942, the British losses due to enemy attack averaged 456,000 tons a month with five months exceeding 500,000 tons. The majority of the attacks took place in the western Atlantic with further losses occurring in the Mediterranean and Arctic. A significant number of the ships sunk were tankers loaded with oil desperately needed to maintain the Allied war effort. The success of the U-boat offensive was not accidental. German signals intelligence had broken the Admiralty's convoy codes providing U-boat captains with the location and anticipated route of each convoy as it made its way across the Atlantic. The worst month for losses was June 1942, with German submarines sinking 124 ships totaling 623,545 tons. If destruction on this scale continued unabated, Britain would soon be defeated.

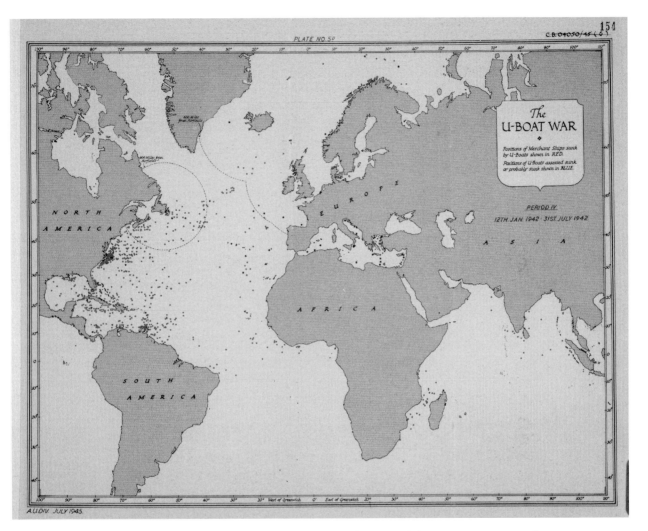

Chart showing the position of merchant ships and U-boats sunk between January to July 1942.
MFQ 1/589 (28)

Salvation occurred in October 1942, when a Sunderland flying boat detected a German submarine operating in the shipping lanes between Port Said and the British naval bases at Haifa in the eastern Mediterranean. The discovery was immediately passed on to the nearest ship in the vicinity, HMS *Hero*, who raced to the last known sighting of the submarine, later identified as *U-559*. HMS *Hero* was soon joined by the destroyers *Dulverton*, *Hawarth*, *Pakenham* and *Petard*. The search for *U-559* lasted all day in a deadly game of hide and seek. In an attempt to bring the submarine to the surface, a barrage of depth charges was unleashed. The force of the explosions cracked the submarine's pressure hull and it began to take on water. The commander

Photograph of a Sunderland flying boat. *CN 11/6 (99)*

of the submarine, Hans Heidtmann, brought *U-559* to the surface and ordered the crew to abandon ship. Fearing that the stricken vessel was about to be scuttled, the German crew jumped overboard without first destroying the Enigma machine or its codebooks. In the ensuing panic, the levers that opened the seawater vents jammed. Unable to flood its tanks, *U-559* remained partially submerged with its conning tower visible above the waves.

In an act of great courage, three crew members from the *Petard* seized the opportunity and boarded the abandoned submarine. Once inside they recovered a code book and short weather cipher. Before they could escape from the submarine, the three sailors were hit by a large wave. Lieutenant Anthony Fasson and Able Seaman Colin Grazier were both drowned and were posthumously awarded the George Cross. The third member of the boarding party was sixteen-year-old Tommy Brown, the *Petard*'s canteen assistant, who had impulsively jumped on board the German submarine on his own initiative. Brown managed to leap from the conning tower before the *U-559* began to capsize and sank below the waves. He was later awarded the George Medal for his courage. It was subsequently discovered that he had lied about his age when joining the navy. He was immediately discharged and returned to his family home in South Shields where he died two years later saving his younger sister from a burning house. The code books and cipher keys salvaged from the *U-559* proved invaluable and enabled codebreakers at Bletchley Park to crack the

Shark cipher. In December 1942, after ten months in the dark, Hut 8 was once again able to read German naval Enigma. With access to U-boat messages restored, convoys were re-routed to avoid the German wolf packs. In total, 105 out of 177 convoys were directed away from U-boat attack areas with British shipping losses dropping dramatically.

The Germans countered these reverses by increasing the numbers of U-boats operating in the Atlantic. This made it more difficult for the Admiralty to re-route convoys into safe areas; avoiding the threat of submarine attack in one sector of the Atlantic brought shipping closer to the next line of U-boats waiting in reserve. Up to this point in the Battle of the Atlantic, the intelligence derived from Enigma had been used primarily to support a defensive strategy in which convoys were re-routed away from known positions of U-boats. In spring 1943, a more offensive posture was adopted. Intelligence derived from Enigma decrypts was used to mount attacks against U-boat refuelling tenders which greatly reduced the time submarines could remain on patrol. To add to German troubles, escort ships and patrol aircraft were being fitted with higher frequency radar that doubled its effective range.

The Italian submarine *Uarsciek* caught in the searchlights of HMS *Petard*. *ADM 199/2060*

By June 1943, U-boats were being sunk faster than they could be replaced, with reported Allied shipping losses at their lowest point since 1941. To avoid the total destruction of the German U-boat fleet, Dönitz was forced to withdraw his submarines from the North Atlantic and station them in the waters off the Azores to be used against US shipping. By 1944, Bletchley Park was reading German naval messages within hours of transmission. In the first three months of 1944, only three merchant ships were sunk with a corresponding loss of 36 U-boats. Even though many submarines remained operational until 1945, it was clear that Germany had already lost the Battle of the Atlantic.

German U-boat attacked off the coast of Spain by an Armstrong Whitworth Whitley aircraft from No. 10 Operational Training Unit, June 1943. *CN 1/39*

A successful attack by Gibraltar aircraft in September, 1943, wrecked this U-Boat and drove it ashore on the north coast of Spanish Morocco. (12th September, 1943).

A stricken U-boat off the North coast of Spanish Morocco, September 1943. *AIR 20/5618*

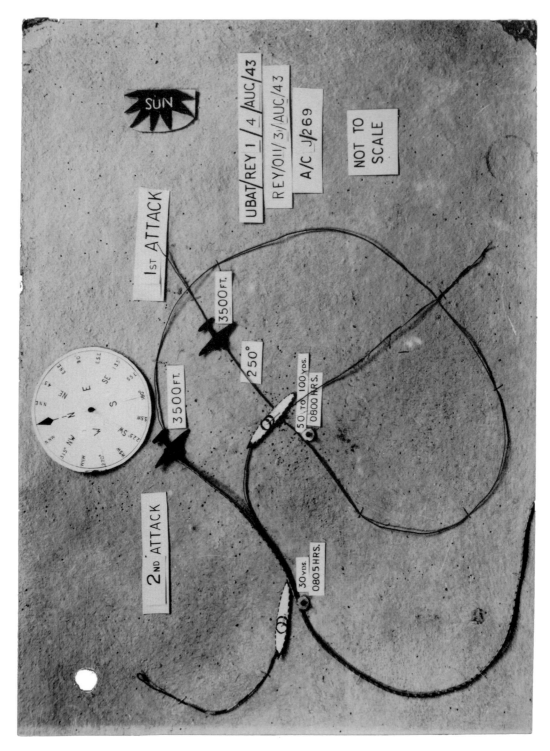

Chart showing depth charge attacks on U-boats in the North Atlantic by Liberator aircraft, August 1943. *ADM 199/1414*

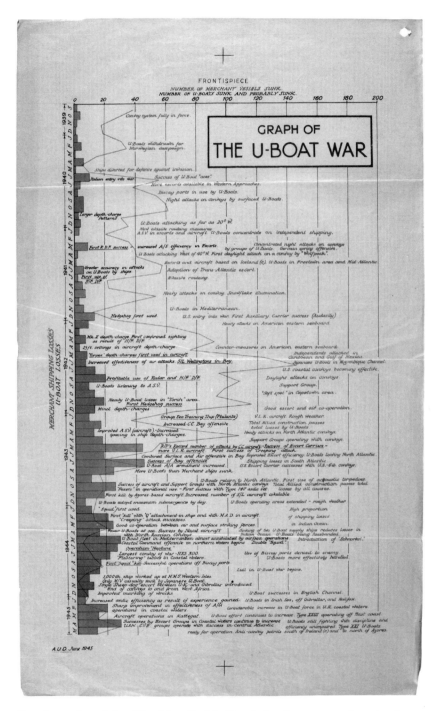

Graph produced by Bletchley Park's Naval Section comparing the losses suffered by U-boats and allied shipping during the war. *HW 18/207*

CHAPTER 5

THE WAR IN THE FAR EAST

On 11 December 1941, four days after Imperial Japan's surprise attack against the US Pacific Fleet based at Pearl Harbor, Nazi Germany declared war on the United States. The pretext for the declaration was America's 'flagrant' violation of the rules of neutrality and its support for declared enemies of the Reich. Later the same day, the US Congress unanimously declared war on Germany. The active involvement of America in the war allowed the two transatlantic allies to exchange military secrets and establish a new era of close Anglo-American cooperation in code breaking and signals intelligence. From the beginning of the war, Churchill had sought an agreement with Roosevelt covering the exchange of information on cryptography and ciphers but US neutrality hindered meaningful collaboration. In January 1941, a select group of military officers, led by Captain Abraham 'Abe' Sinkov of the US Army's Signals Intelligence Service, visited Britain. The delegation was shown around Bletchley Park and exchanged information on German and Japanese systems.

The British were particularly interested in the security of Japanese ciphers and discovering to what extent US codebreakers had managed to read diplomatic or military telegrams transmitted between Tokyo and its missions abroad. The US revealed that initial work on breaking Japanese diplomatic ciphers had begun in the mid-1930s, when US cryptographers noticed a flaw in the Japanese machine cipher known as Angooki Type A. This cipher was used by the Japanese foreign ministry to communicate with its missions abroad and was given the code name 'Red'. In early 1939, the Japanese upgraded their ciphers and adopted the Type B machine which was given the designation 'Purple' by US cryptographers. The deciphered and translated product distributed to military commands was code named 'Magic'. The new cipher machine was installed in major Japanese embassies abroad including Berlin, Rome, London and Washington. The Purple cipher was soon broken, enabling a working version of the machine to be constructed by US code beakers in September 1940. A copy of the machine, in addition to a German codebook and some Mexican ciphers, were handed over to the British during Sinkov's visit to Bletchley Park. In return, the British divulged a substantial amount of information on German, Italian and Russian ciphers.

TOP SECRET "U"

NAVAL SECTION   ULTRA/ZIP/SJA/2302

JNA 20   C/S 736

TOO 042000 August 1941 [Note 1941]

From: YAYOI [3rd Dept. (Intelligence) IHQNS] TOKYO

To :   JNA MEXICO

[WARNING ABOUT NIIKAWA]

A certain NIIKAWA (新 川) was in WASHINGTON recently and tried to get in touch with our Attaché there. It is feared that he was intimidated by the Americans after the TACHIBANA incident and that he may be doing counter-espionage for them. It was considered dangerous for an attaché to have dealings with such a man in AMERICA, and the attaché in WASHINGTON was instructed to refuse to have anything to do with him. As he may therefore get in touch with you, you are requested to adopt the following course of action.

1.   Since it is not considered dangerous for him to be at your post, you should have him stay in some suitable place [? for a short time] and find out whether he is acting in good faith [or] whether he is doing counter-espionage, and whether he is being trailed by the Americans.

2.   You should draw up a new plan for future operations.

3.   In dealing with him, you should take great care to preserve secrecy and to guard against counter-espionage.

4.   He has not been paid his remuneration for this year, and so will probably ask for it. I would be grateful if you would not pay him at once, but [first] inform the head of the 3rd Department.

5.   He is 50 years old of about medium build, broad-shouldered, with thinning hair and his cheeks are

Continued . . .

Decrypt of Japanese naval message sent from Tokyo to Mexico, August 1941. *HW 23/354 (2302)*

HEAD.
D. & R.

MOST SECRET.

TO BE KEPT UNDER LOCK AND KEY: NEVER TO BE REMOVED FROM THE OFFICE.

JAPANESE POLICY: NOTIFICATION TO GERMAN AND ITALIAN

GOVERNMENTS.

B.J. 62.

No: 092889

Date: 4th July, 1941.

From: Foreign Minister, TOKYO.

To: Japanese Ambassador, BERLIN.

No: 585 Urgent.

Date: 2nd July, 1941.

At a conference in the forenoon of the 2nd the main features of Japanese national policy were decided on, and on the basis of that decision the German and Italian Ambassadors were asked to come and see me the same afternoon and a notification was made to them as in my immediately following telegram No. 584. [Not received].

My separate telegram No.585 [below] is the text in English, and the text addressed to ITALY is identical in content.

Please repeat this telegram and Nos.584 and 585 to our Ambassador in ROME. I have repeated to MOSCOW.

MATSUOKA.

No: 585 of 2nd July, 1941.

[Dept: Note: Text in English exactly as cyphered].

Oral Statement (Translation):

Please convey the following to His Excellency Herrn von RIBBENTROP:

I have duly noted Your Excellency's request made through Ambassador General OTT in TOKYO and

Ambassador

Director (3).
F.O. (3).
P.I.D.
Admiralty.
War Office (3).
India Office.
Colonial Office.
Ministry.
Morton.
Bridges.

Decrypt of diplomatic communications between Tokyo and Berlin.
HW 12/265 (92889-1)

The British were reluctant to reveal the true extent of their work on Enigma and it is uncertain how much information was provided to the American delegation. The British were particularly concerned about US security protocols. It was feared that if sensitive information was handed over to the Americans, it would inadvertently reveal that the British had broken the Enigma codes and were reading German military communications. If British fears were realized, the consequences would be profound. The security breach would enable Germany to deploy new ciphers and deprive Britain of a vital source of intelligence during a crucial stage of the war. The official record of the Sinkov visit indicates that no details of Enigma were provided to the US delegation. However, a subsequent US report states that following the personal intervention of Winston Churchill, British successes against Enigma were disclosed to members of the mission on the proviso that they gave a pledge of secrecy. The American delegation were also required to forward a list of names to the British authorities detailing the individuals with whom they intended to share the information. They further agreed not to add anyone to the list without obtaining prior British permission. Only after accepting these stringent conditions were the Americans allowed full access to the work on Enigma. To further emphasize the need for absolute secrecy, the American delegation was not allowed to take notes nor were they provided with any information on paper.

In June 1941, the Anglo-American relationship in the Far East was further consolidated when both countries agreed to pool signals intelligence gathered by the British base at Singapore and the US Pacific Fleet. In August, Alastair Denniston, Britain's chief code breaker, visited Washington and agreed to the exchange of liaison officers between Bletchley Park and Arlington Hall, a former girls' school in Virginia, requisitioned by the US military to house the headquarters of the US Signals Intelligence Service. It was not until America's entry into the war, however, that full-scale cooperation between the two countries was formally established. The British were keen to establish a division of effort, with the Americans focusing on Japanese ciphers in the Pacific leaving the British to concentrate on German and Italian systems in the Atlantic and Mediterranean. Despite the close cooperation between the two countries, the British were still reticent to share full details of Enigma with the US authorities and sought to curtail the Americans from duplicating British efforts.

The American navy was unwilling to accept British primacy in the battle of the Atlantic. By 1942, US merchant ships were being sunk off the American coast and in the North Atlantic in increasing numbers. The US Congress demanded immediate action. Intelligence on the location and activity of German U-boats was received from British sources but the intercepted traffic remained a closely guarded secret. In February 1942, the German navy introduced of a new cipher system for communicating with its U-boat fleet in the North Atlantic. As described in Chapter Four, the new cipher employed a special Enigma

HW 1/6

MOST SECRET

C/6863.

LONDON,

24th June, 1941.

PRIME MINISTER.

After considering, from all angles, the possibility of divulging to the President the information regarding U.S. Naval Units being chased by U. Boats, I find myself unable to devise any safe means of wrapping up the information in a manner which would not imperil this source, which should, without fail, play a vital part in the Battle of the Atlantic.

The fact that the message in question was passed by the Admiral Commanding U. Boats to submarines actually operating, renders it well nigh impossible that the information could have been secured by an agent, and however much we insist that it came from a highly placed source, I greatly doubt the enemy being for a moment deceived, should there be any indiscretion in the U.S.A. That this might occur, cannot be ruled out, as the Americans are not in any sense as security minded as one would wish, and I need only draw your attention to the attached cutting from to-day's "Daily Express", on a matter which, in my opinion, should not have been made public if the two Secret Services are to work together as closely as is imperative.

It is true that the American experts who visited the United Kingdom gave us a very valuable insight into Japanese cryptographic methods, but they, themselves, impressed upon me how cautious they were in passing any of the results to the State Department.

At a recent Meeting of the Chiefs of Staff, it was agreed that information derived from this Most Secret source should only be communicated to the U.S. Naval and Military Authorities when we were satisfied that the source was not endangered. I believe that any other decision as regards weakening the veil of secrecy would cause the greatest regret at a later date, and I similarly hold the view that it would be fatal to divulge to the Russians immediate information which we are securing about German operational intentions on the Eastern Front. To be of any value, it would mean that the information would be immediately transmitted to the Commanders

in/

Letter from Stewart Menzies, the Chief of MI6, to Churchill expressing his concern over sharing Ultra material with the United States and Russia. *HW 1/6*

machine, the Triton M4, which was equipped with an extra rotor. British codebreakers were unable to break the new cipher, with appalling results. The lack of intelligence meant that the Royal Navy could not re-route convoys to safe areas allowing U-boats to attack Allied shipping at will. The introduction of the new cipher, known as Shark, made Britain's refusal to share Enigma intelligence with the Americans impossible to justify. In April, with losses mounting, the British were informed that unless it released everything it knew about naval Enigma to the US Navy, America would go it alone. The British subsequently agreed to supply the technical information required but sought to delay the final agreement.

To break the new cipher, reliance was placed on the next generation of high speed 'bombes'. The United States was the only country that possessed the money and scientific manpower needed to develop the technology in the timescale required. Increasingly tired of British obfuscation, the US Navy was determined to possess its own codebreaking bombe. In August 1942, Captain Edward Hastings, Bletchley Park's liaison officer in America, was informed that the US Navy was soon to embark on an extensive research programme to develop a high-speed bombe. To demonstrate its resolve, a contract was signed with the National Cash Register Company with an allocated budget of over $2m. The British were concerned that the US Navy was planning to curtail all meaningful cooperation in signals intelligence unless Britain was willing to offer something in return. To prevent a schism developing in the Anglo-American relationship, the head of Bletchley Park's naval section, Commander Edward 'Jumbo' Travis, travelled to Washington for exploratory talks. The result was the so-called Holden Agreement, named after the US director of naval communications, Captain Carl Holden which was signed between the two countries on 2 October 1942.

The Holden Agreement formally sanctioned the exchange of information covering the interception and exploitation of Allied signals intelligence. The Americans were the main beneficiaries. In return for full partnership in the Atlantic against German naval ciphers, including the pooling of all intercepted traffic, keys and cribs, the US navy was given sole direction and control over Japanese communications. Britain agreed to withdraw from active codebreaking work in the Pacific area and to disband the British-Australian naval unit stationed at Melbourne. The agreement soon came to the attention of the US Army, who sought to establish a parallel stream of raw Enigma intercepts covering the German army and air force. Negotiations continued until May 1943, when agreement was eventually reached between Travis and the head of US military intelligence, General George V. Strong, providing for the complete exchange of intelligence relating to enemy ciphers and codes. The agreement reflected the practical realities; responsibility for reading Japanese army and air force ciphers was given to the United States, with the British responsible for deciphering German and Italian army and air force traffic. In January 1944, Allied signals cooperation was consolidated further when both countries signed the BRUSA agreement establishing a global network of stations sited in Washington, Bletchley Park, Pearl Harbor, Melbourne and Colombo. The agreement also contained provisions covering the exchange of personnel and security protocols safeguarding the handling of Ultra and Magic material and its distribution.

The intelligence gained by breaking the Japanese diplomatic cipher Purple was of crucial importance for the success of the D-Day landings. Particular significance was placed on the content of the messages exchanged between the Japanese embassy in Berlin and the foreign ministry in Tokyo. The reports compiled by the Japanese military attaché were particularly

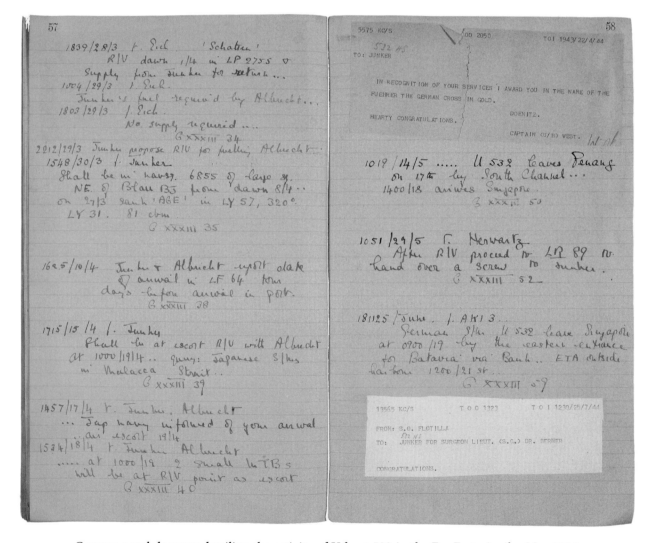

German naval decrypts detailing the activity of U-boat 532 in the Far East, April – May 1944.
HW 18/371 (57,58)

M. FORM No. 1479

TOP ~~MOST~~ SECRET ULTRA

TO BE KEPT UNDER LOCK AND KEY AND NEVER TO BE REMOVED FROM THE OFFICE.
THIS FORM IS TO BE USED FOR AIR INTELLIGENCE MESSAGES ONLY.

NR. No.	GR. No.		OFFICE SERIAL No.
DATE	TIME OF RECEIPT	TIME OF DESPATCH	SYSTEM
TO:			
FROM:			
SENDERS No.			

PAGE FOUR.   CX/MSS/T183/84 (CONTINUED).
----------   ----------------------------

ENEMY MINING FROM THE AIR REMAINED LIVELY WITH SCHWERPUNKT
OFF SUBMARINE BASES, LEZARDRIEUX AND AGAINST CHANNEL ISLAND
NARROWS. AGENTS' REPORTS, APART FROM A PLETHORA OF LANDING
DATES WHICH MAINLY POINT TO THE FIRST HALF OF MAY, YIELDED NO
SPECIAL INFORMATION.

C. IN C. WEST APPRECIATES THE SITUATION AS FOLLOWS:

INVASION-PREPARATIONS BY THE ANGLO-AMERICANS IN THE ENGLISH
MOTHERLAND ARE COMPLETED. DESPITE THE FACT THAT VISUAL AND
PHOTO RECCE HAS NOT YET BEEN ABLE TO INCLUDE THE WHOLE OF THE
ENGLISH SOUTH COAST, THE OBSERVED CONCENTRATIONS OF LANDING
SHIPPING SPACE, ESPECIALLY IN THE AREA NORTH OF THE ISLE OF WIGHT
(PORTSMOUTH - SOUTHAMPTON), NEVERTHELESS GIVE A CLEAR PICTURE OF
A MAIN CONCENTRATION DEFINING ITSELF IN THAT AREA. TONNAGE OF
SHIPPING SPACE FOR LANDINGS WHICH HAS SO FAR BEEN OBSERVED CAN BE
ASSUMED TO BE SUFFICIENT FOR 12 TO 13 DIVISIONS (WITHOUT HEAVY
EQUIPMENT AND REAR ELEMENTS) FOR FAIRLY SHORT SEA-ROUTES.
TAKEN ALTOGETHER, AND INCLUDING AN ESTIMATE OF THE CAPACITY OF THE
OTHER ENGLISH SOUTH-COAST HARBOURS WHICH HAVE SO FAR NOT BEEN

DISTRIBUTION:			
DEGREE OF PRIORITY	TIME OF ORIGIN	SIGNATURE OF ORIGINATOR, NOT TO BE TELEPRINTED	OPERATOR'S RECEIPT

Ultra decrypt showing German expectations of the timing and location of the Allied invasion of Europe, May 1944. *HW 1/2874*

illuminating. Written between 1943 and 1944, the reports contained detailed accounts of the beach defences being installed by the German army, including insights into when and where the German High Command expected the Allied invasion of Europe to take place. The messages revealed that although German commanders were expecting a landing in Normandy, this was believed to be a diversion to draw troops away from the main Allied landing at the Pas de Calais. The information derived from these sources allowed the western allies to prepare countermeasures and reassured Churchill and the Chiefs of Staff that Hitler expected the main invasion to take place at Calais rather than at Normandy. This intelligence was fed into the planning for Operation Fortitude, the code name for the deception strategy employed by the Allies during the build-up to the 1944 D-Day landings.

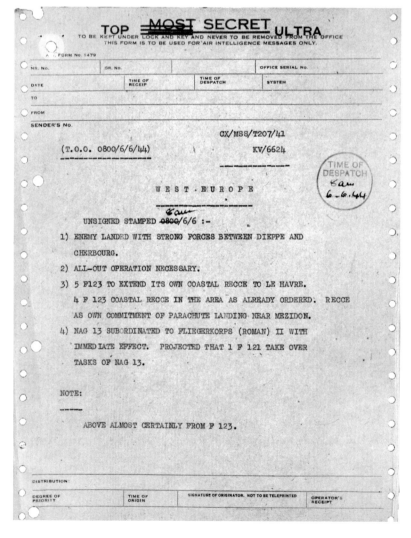

D-Day intercept.
HW 1/2893

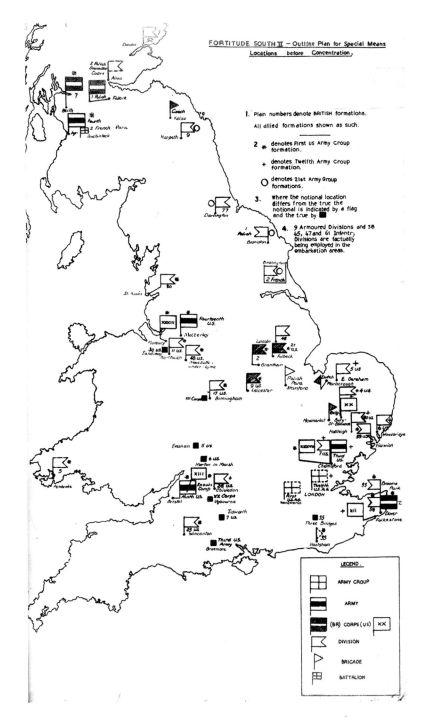

Map showing location of fictious army units as part of Operation Fortitude. *WO 208/4374*

World War II poster – The War against Japan. *INF 13/213 (46)*

CHAPTER 6

ALAN TURING

The success of Allied codebreakers in intercepting and decrypting enemy communications is estimated to have shortened the war by two years. During the course of the war, the number of people engaged in code breaking and the interception of enemy communications increased dramatically. By 1945 and the defeat of Nazi Germany, the total number of staff stationed at Bletchley Park and its outstations at Gayhurst Manor, Wavendon House and Eastcote had grown from approximately 150 in 1939 to over 8,500 codebreakers and clerical staff by 1945. Not all staff working at Bletchley Park were mathematicians and linguists, many undertook manual and repetitive tasks including compiling card indexes, transcribing messages and operating machinery. One of the first to report for duty at Bletchley Park, was Alan Turing, who is now widely regarded as one of the most influential computer scientists of the twentieth century.

Born on 23 June 1912 in Maida Vale, London, Turing's early childhood was spent in East Sussex. His father served in the Indian Civil Service and his parents were often overseas, leaving Alan and his brother John to stay with a retired army couple in Hastings on the south coast. They lived a solitary life and only saw their parents occasionally when they returned home to Britain on leave. Turing was educated at Hazelhurst preparatory school, three miles south of Tunbridge Wells, and at Sherborne, an independent boarding school in Dorset, where he began to reveal his remarkable knowledge and understanding of complex mathematical subjects. In 1931, Turing won a scholarship to King's College, Cambridge and was awarded a first-class honours degree in mathematics. At the age of 22, he was elected a fellow of King's College.

Turing's research at King's revolved around computable numbers and the *Entscheidungsproblem* (decision problem) first postulated by the German mathematician David Hilbert in 1928. In simple terms, this posed the question whether mathematical statements or algorithms could be proved true or false under all circumstances. In attempting to provide an answer to this question, Turing conceived the concept of the universal machine – now known as the Turing machine – which could perform an infinite number of tasks with each task following a specific set of instructions. Turing's ideas were published in 1936 in the *Proceedings of the London Mathematical Society* and are now widely recognized as laying the foundations of modern computer theory. In 1936, Turing was invited to study at Princeton University in America where he began to explore cryptography and found the time to construct an electromechanical binary multiplier capable of encoding (and decoding) complex mathematical functions.

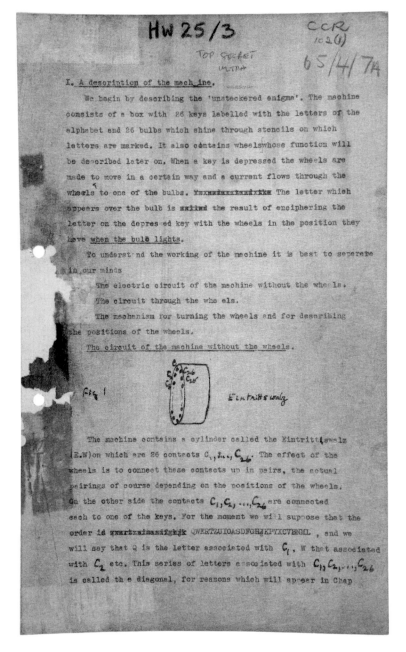

Four pages of text detailing the mathematical theory of the Enigma machine by Alan Turing (4 pages of text). *HW 25/3 (1), HW 25/3 (5), HW 25/3 (69), and HW 25/3 (81)*

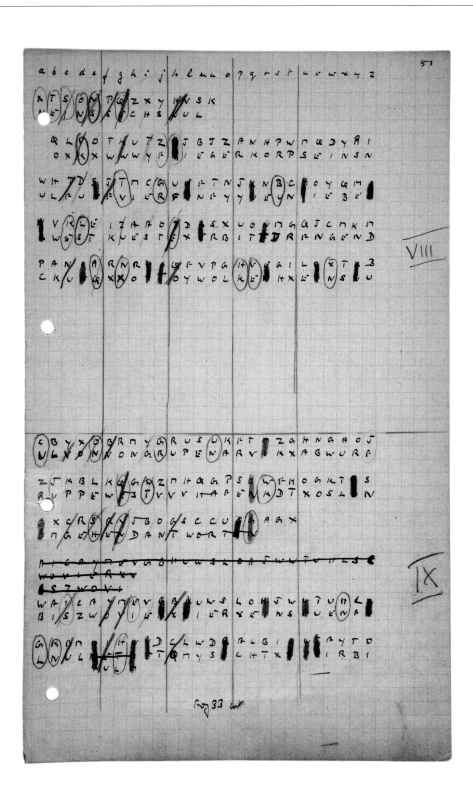

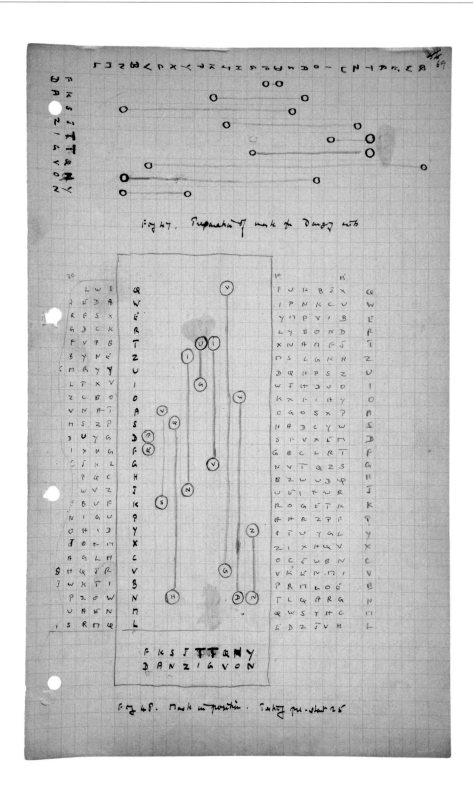

Fig 47. Preparation of mask for Danzig nets

Fig 48. Mask in position. Setting pre-start 25

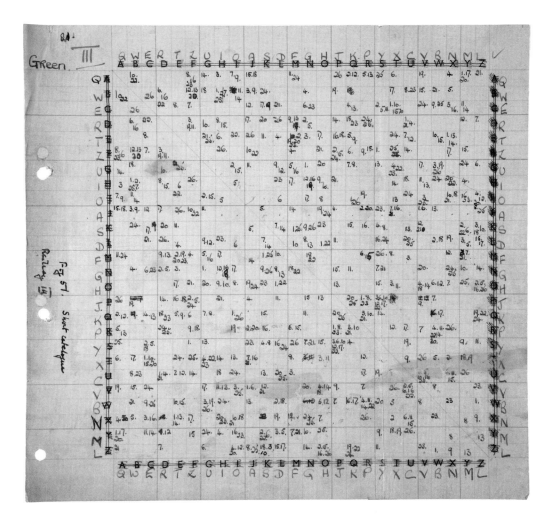

In 1938, with the German invasion of Czechoslovakia seemingly imminent and a future European war a distinct possibility, Turing returned to Cambridge University where he undertook secret work for the Government Code and Cypher School. Following the outbreak of war, Turing was one of the first recruits to report to Bletchley Park. On his arrival there, Turing was given responsibility for breaking the German naval Enigma. The work was undertaken in Hut 8 in the grounds of Bletchley where he remained for the next 18 months. Working closely with Dilly Knox, a fellow King's College alumnus and Chief Cryptographer at GC&CS, Turing began to construct an electro-mechanical machine that could calculate both the wheel settings and plugboard connections of any Enigma machine used by the Germans at any given time. The machine was known as the 'bombe' and bore similarities to the Polish bomba. Both machines consisted of a series of Enigma machines wired together to determine whether a particular setting was possible. To operate effectively, however, the Polish machine depended on indicator procedures that the Germans could change at any moment. In contrast, Turing's bombe was a more general-purpose machine that relied on crib-based decryption.

A crib was a short piece of text the meaning of which could be guessed or inferred. This was not as difficult as first imagined. German military communications followed regimented guidelines with the same words and phrases occurring at the beginning and end of messages and reports. The transmission of daily weather reports proved a valuable source. These messages

Paper on the Statistics of Repetitions by Alan Turing.
HW 25/38 (1)

We now turn to the problem of calculating the probability of a given fit when we know the proportion $\overset{\alpha_r}{/}$ of regramme cards in the urn for each r. The calculation is going to be slightly complicated by the convention which we introduced, that not all drawings can lead to a comparison. We have therefore to calculate the proportion of draws which lead to a comparison, i.e. in which the length does not overshoot the mark. The answer is that as the length of overlap tends to infinity the proportion tends to $\dfrac{1}{1+\Sigma r\alpha_r}$; in the case of hatted material this is $\dfrac{25}{26}$.

Now put $A = 1 - \Sigma\alpha_r$. Consider a repetition figure in which there are k_r r-grammes. Let the overlap be L. The number of ~~draws which give no repeat is~~ 'no repeat' cards drawn is $L+1-\Sigma(r+1)k_r$. The proportion of right draws which are relevant is

$$A^{L+1-\Sigma(r+1)k_r}\;\overset{\infty}{\underset{r=1}{\prod}}\;\alpha_r^{k_r}$$

and the proportion of the right <u>comparisons</u> which are relevant is (assuming L reasonably large)

$$\left(1+\Sigma r\alpha_r\right)A^{L+1-\Sigma(r+1)k_r}\;\overset{\infty}{\underset{r=1}{\prod}}\;\alpha_r^{k_r}$$

Similarly calculating with the urn whose proportions were made up from hatted material we find for the proportion of wrong comparisons which are relevant

$$\frac{26}{25}\left(\frac{25}{26}\right)^{L+1-\Sigma(r+1)k_r}\;\overset{\infty}{\underset{r=1}{\prod}}\left(\frac{25}{26^{r+1}}\right)^{k_r}$$

Hence the odds[*] on our fit are

$$q=\lambda\,\frac{25(1+\Sigma r\alpha_r)}{26}\left(\frac{26A}{25}\right)^{L+1-\Sigma(r+1)k_r}\;\overset{\infty}{\underset{r=1}{\prod}}\left(\frac{26^{r+1}\alpha_r}{25}\right)^{k_r}$$

where λ is the a priori odds. This is most conveniently written as

$$\log q = \log\lambda + \Sigma\mu_r k_r - \nu L + \log(1-\Sigma\alpha_r)(1+\Sigma r\alpha_r)$$

where $\mu_r = \log\dfrac{k_r 26^{r+1}}{25} - (r+1)\log\dfrac{26A}{25}$ and $\nu = \log\dfrac{25}{26A} \fallingdotseq \Sigma\alpha_r - 2/51$

$-\Sigma r\alpha_r$

---

[*]The odds on an event are defined to be the probability of the event divided by the probability of its negation

Paper on the Statistics of Repetitions by Alan Turing. *HW 25/39 (7)*

always began with the term *wettervorhersage* (weather forecast) followed by the location of the weather ship e.g. Biscay or Brittany. Moreover, as the weather conditions at each location were known, other aspects of the message – sunny, raining, cloudy – could be inferred. Another common example was the term *fortsetzung* (continuation of previous message) which was invariably used if the message was sent in several sections. Once a crib had been obtained, it could be used to match up pairs of letters by exploiting the fact that the Enigma machine never encoded a letter as itself. This information allowed the bombe to determine which settings were incorrect and could be ignored. This reduced the thousands of possible combinations of rotors and plug boards to a manageable number that could be tested manually.

The use of cribs was enhanced by additional information gathered from captured enemy documents. One of the first of these 'pinches' occurred in April 1940 during the Norway campaign when the destroyer HMS *Griffin* apprehended what appeared to be a Dutch fishing boat called the *Polares*. On closer examination, it soon became apparent that the boat was not an innocent fishing vessel but a heavily armed German trawler the *Schiff 26* transporting ammunition and supplies to the German forces occupying Norway. The boat was ordered to stop and surrender its crew and cargo to British forces. Before the trawler was boarded, however, various documents and communication equipment, including an Enigma machine, were thrown into the sea by the crew. Most sank to the bottom, but a significant number of documents were recovered from the surface including an Enigma operator's logbook, some scraps of cipher text and details of the plugboard settings. The captured documents were sent to Bletchley and enabled Turing to calibrate his bombes to break the naval Enigma code for that day.

The celebrations were short lived as the recovered documents only provided the key for a five-day period between 22 to 27 April 1940. To maintain the security of its communications, the German navy changed its Enigma settings on a regular basis. To discover the new settings, Turing had to find another way of working out the position of the rotors without relying on the use of captured documents. One method devised by Turing was called Banburismus, which exploited the principle of sequential analysis to infer the probable settings used by the Enigma machine. The procedure relied on comparing two messages to look for repeated sequences. The process was made easier by punching the messages onto thin cards and laying the two message-cards on top of each other over a light-source. If two holes were aligned and light was able to shine straight through, this indicated a repeated sequence. This light technique pioneered by Turing made it much simpler for codebreakers at Bletchley to detect and count the repeated sequences. The information gained in this way could be used to rule out certain arrangements of Enigma rotors and significantly reduce the time required to test possible settings on the bombes. The cards used in the process were printed in Banbury in Oxfordshire hence the name Banbarismus.

Following America's entry into the war in December 1941, codebreakers on both sides of the Atlantic were able to establish full scale cooperation. To explore what progress had been made by American cryptographers, Turing travelled to New York to spend time at the Bell Labs building on Manhattan's Lower West Side. Turing arrived in America in November 1942 and immediately began work into encrypted speech signals. He also visited the headquarters of the US Navy codebreakers in Washington to compare notes on the next generation of bombes.

On his return to Bletchley, Turing was appointed scientific consultant and continued his work on encrypted speech systems. This work was conducted at Hanslope Park in Buckinghamshire in conjunction with the Radio Security Service and resulted in a secure voice communication device codenamed Delilah. Turing also devised a new technique, known as Turingery, which was deployed against the Lonenz cipher machine used by the German High Command. The statistical technique pioneered by Turing allowed the position of the teleprinter's rotor wheels to be determined. More importantly, the process could be replicated and used on Collossus, the world's first programmable computer built by Tommy Flowers, an engineer working at the Post Office Research Station at Dollis Hill in north-west London. The speed of Colossus combined with the genius of Turing allowed codebreakers to read Hitler's orders to his generals until Allied victory in May 1945. In recognition of his work at Bletchley Park, Turing was awarded an OBE.

Photograph of the Delilah coding machine used for secure speech communications. *HW 25/36*

Following the end of the war, Turing took up a position at the National Physical Laboratory in Teddington where he worked on a design for a stored-programme electronic computer. The machine was christened ACE (automatic computing engine) and was developed in response to the US Army's computer project known as ENIAC (Electronic Numerical Integrator and Computer). Although both projects had similarities, the concept proposed by Turing was more advanced and versatile than its American counterpart, due to its ability to operate using stored programmes. Because of the difficulty of securing funding and equipment in post-war Britain, the first version of the ACE that was built was a less ambitious version compared to Turing's original design. The prototype ACE ran its first programme on 10 May 1950 and, at the time, was widely regarded as the fastest computer in the world. Many of the features developed in ACE were later incorporated into the English Electric DEUCE computer and laid the foundations of the modern computer industry.

In 1948, Turing was appointed Deputy Director of the Manchester University Computing Laboratory where he continued his work on stored-programme computers. He also began to experiment with artificial intelligence and was one of the first to ask the question whether machines could think. To address this problem, he developed the Turing test as a means of distinguishing between humans and machines. In 1952, Turing was charged with an act of 'gross indecency' with a young man, to which he pleaded guilty. Rather than face a prison term (homosexuality was illegal in the UK until 1967) he agreed to 'chemical castration' administered by regular injections of oestrogen. His conviction led to the removal of his security clearance and he was denied entry to the United States.

On 8 June 1954, he was found dead at his home in Wilmslow, Cheshire. An inquest determined that he had taken his own life. In September 2009, the British Prime Minister, Gordon Brown, apologized for the treatment given to Turing during his lifetime and in 2013 Turing was officially pardoned. The Policing and Crime Act enacted in 2017, contains legislation that retrospectively exonerates other men convicted of similar offences; it is widely known as Turing's law. In July 2019, it was revealed that Alan Turing will appear on the new £50 polymer banknote. The decision was announced by the Governor of the Bank of England who stated that Turing was the father of computer science and artificial intelligence and a giant on whose shoulders so many now stand. The banknote contains a quote from Turing given to *The Times* newspaper in 1949 describing his early work into computer technology which reads: 'This is only a foretaste of what is to come, and a shadow of what is going to be.'

CHAPTER 7

POST WAR DEVELOPMENTS

The war-time success of the codebreakers at Bletchley Park was tempered by the realization that the organization – now known as the Government Communications Headquarters (GCHQ) – was not free to determine its own priorities but was reliant on its parent body, the Secret Intelligence Service (MI6), for the provision of money, personnel and accommodation. This dependency rankled with senior staff, especially as MI6 had not covered itself with glory during the Second World War. In September 1944, following the liberation of Paris, a group of senior codebreakers met in private to discuss the future direction of their organization. The group was led by Gordon Welchman, the head of Hut 6, the section at Bletchley Park responsible for breaking German army and air force Enigma ciphers. Welchman, who was known and respected for his organizational skills, advocated the creation of a new civilian body, independent from MI6, to be responsible for all signals intelligence in the UK and overseas. He also suggested that all available resources should be focused on developing computer technology and state-of-the-art communications equipment rather than devoting time and resources against the Japanese which was largely an American concern.

It was widely recognized in government that signals intelligence and the ability to intercept and read the communications of other states would play a significant role in the post-war world. The concern expressed by Welchman and his fellow codebreakers was that GCHQ would not receive sufficient funds to attract the best computer scientists and technicians that were needed to achieve these ambitious plans. The secret nature of GCHQ's work was also its worst enemy as very few people outside of a small circle were aware of the magnitude of its wartime achievements or its potential to support British diplomatic and military objectives on a global basis. These arguments found a receptive audience with the British Chiefs of Staff, who were more aware than most of GCHQ's contribution to Allied victory. Churchill was a staunch supporter of Bletchley and apparently told George VI that Ultra had effectively won the war. Meeting in November 1945, following the defeat of Germany and Japan, the Chiefs attempted to devise a military strategy which addressed the uncertainties of the new world order. In terms of new technology, atomic energy, computers, radar and signals intelligence were given top priory. Despite receiving the support of the military's top brass, staff numbers at GCHQ fell dramatically following demobilization from a wartime strength of 8,900 to a projected figure of 1,000 for 1946. The army's interception stations also underwent significant reductions, with staff numbers falling from a peak of 4,000 personnel in December 1945 to fewer than 1,000 by the following March.

In April 1946, British codebreakers were re-located from their war-time headquarters at Bletchley Park to Eastcote in north-west London situated close to the Post Office Research Department at Dollis Hill. In comparison to Bletchley, the facilities at Eastcote were cramped and unattractive. The move to London was also a realization of the organization's ambition to be an independent body when, following a review of post-war intelligence, it was removed from the orbit of MI6 and placed under the control of the Foreign Office. To mark its new status, the organization took the war-time cover name of GCHQ as its official title. The first director of GCHQ was Sir Edward Wilfred Travis who had replaced Denniston as operation head of Bletchley Park in 1942. One of the first tasks undertaken by Travis was to establish a network of listening stations throughout the Commonwealth linking London, Canada, Australia and New Zealand. He was also determined to build and strengthen the good working relationship with the United States. This ambition was shared by senior officials in Washington and reached its culmination soon after the end of the war with the implementation of the UK-US Security Agreement – better known as the 'Five Eyes' or UKUSA agreement. Signed by representatives of the London Signals Intelligence Board and its American counterpart in March 1946, the UKUSA Agreement is without parallel in the Western intelligence world and formed the basis for co-operation between the two countries throughout the Cold War.

The Eastcote site was formerly a war-time outstation of Bletchley Park and housed some of the bombes used to decode German Enigma messages. At its height, a total of 100 machines were operated at Eastcote, controlled by 800 Wrens and 100 RAF technicians. At the end of the war, the bombes were dismantled and the site became known as the London Signals Intelligence Centre. To assist Travis in his task, two deputies were appointed, Nigel de Grey, responsible for operational matters, training and security and Captain Edward Hastings, charged with the management of GCHQ's overseas stations including liaison with the US and Commonwealth countries. The post-war work undertaken at Eastcote focused largely on the Soviet Union and Eastern Europe with the Joint Intelligence Committee directing British codebreakers to concentrate on the Soviet Union's atomic, biological and chemical warfare programmes. The facilitates at Eastcote were only intended as a temporary measure and in 1952 it moved to the outskirts of Cheltenham occupying two sites at Oakley and Benhall formerly used by the Ministry of Pensions.

The move to Cheltenham took place between 1952 and 1954 and fortuitously for GCHQ coincided with the re-armament programme initiated by the British government following the outbreak of the Korean War in the early 1950s. In addition to an increase in resources, the Korean War also resulted in the creation of the National Security Agency, the American equivalent of GCHQ. To remain in close contact with government departments in London, the security section of GCHQ remained at Eastcote. In March 1954, it became a separate independent organization known as the London Communications Security Agency and given responsibility for providing the British government and military with advice and assistance on maintaining the security of its communications and cipher systems. In the mid-1950s, GCHQ also took over control of the Joint Technical Language Service and was given responsibility for electronic intelligence. To facilitate this work, it established the Composite Signals Organization which eventually took over control of the individual networks run by the three armed services. Throughout the Cold War, GCHQ maintained a London office at Palmer Street in Westminster, opposite St James' Park tube station, from where it provided a steady stream of intelligence to its customers in government and the armed forces and consolidated its position as one of the world's leading intelligence agencies.

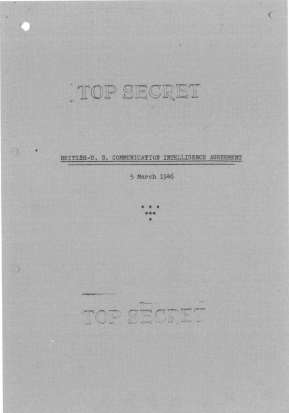

British-US Communication Intelligence Agreement, 1946. *HW 80/4*

TOP SECRET

OUTLINE OF

BRITISH-U. S. COMMUNICATION INTELLIGENCE AGREEMENT

1. Parties to the Agreement

2. Scope of the Agreement

3. Extent of the Agreement - Products

4. Extent of the Agreement - Methods and Techniques

5. Third Parties to the Agreement

6. The Dominions

7. Channels between U. S. and British Empire Agencies

8. Dissemination and Security

9. Dissemination and Security - Commercial

10. Previous Agreements

11. Amendment and Termination of Agreement

12. Activation and Implementation of Agreement

1

TOP SECRET

TOP SECRET

BRITISH-U. S. COMMUNICATION INTELLIGENCE AGREEMENT

1. Parties to the Agreement

The following agreement is made between the State-Army-Navy Communication Intelligence Board (STANCIB) (representing the U. S. State, Navy, and War Departments and all other U. S. Communication Intelligence[1] authorities which may function) and the London Signal Intelligence (SIGINT) Board (representing the Foreign Office, Admiralty, War Office, Air Ministry, and all other British Empire[2] Communication Intelligence authorities which may function).

2. Scope of the Agreement

The agreement governs the relations of the above-mentioned parties in Communication Intelligence matters only. However, the exchange of such collateral material as is applicable for technical purposes and is not prejudicial to national interests will be effected between the Communication Intelligence agencies in both countries.

---

[1]Throughout this agreement Communication Intelligence is understood to comprise all processes involved in the collection, production, and dissemination of information derived from the communications of other nations.

[2]For the purposes of this agreement British Empire is understood to mean all British territory other than the Dominions.

2

TOP SECRET

TOP SECRET

3. Extent of the Agreement - Products

(a) The parties agree to the exchange of the products of the following operations relating to foreign communications:3

(1) collection of traffic

(2) acquisition of communication documents and equipment

(3) traffic analysis

(4) cryptanalysis

(5) decryption and translation

(6) acquisition of information regarding communication organizations, practices, procedures, and equipment

---

3Throughout this agreement foreign communications are understood to mean all communications of the government or of any military, air, or naval force, faction, party, department, agency, or bureau of a foreign country, or of any person or persons acting or purporting to act therefor, and shall include   communications of a foreign country which may contain information of military, political, or economic value. Foreign country as used herein is understood to include any country, whether or not its government is recognized by the U. S. or the British Empire, excluding only the U. S., the British Commonwealth of Nations, and the British Empire.

3

TOP SECRET

TOP SECRET

(b)   Such exchange will be unrestricted on all
work undertaken except when specifically excluded
from the agreement at the request of either party
and with the agreement of the other. It is the intention of each party to limit such exceptions to
the absolute minimum and to exercise no restrictions
other than those reported and mutually agreed upon.

4.   Extent of the Agreement - Methods and Techniques

(a)   The parties agree to the exchange of information regarding methods and techniques involved
in the operations outlined in paragraph 3(a).

(b)   Such exchange will be unrestricted on all
work undertaken, except that upon notification of
the other party information may be withheld by either
party when its special interests so require. Such
notification will include a description of the information being withheld, sufficient in the opinion
of the withholding party, to convey its significance.
It is the intention of each party to limit such exceptions to the absolute minimum.

5.   Third Parties to the Agreement

Both parties will regard this agreement as pre-
cluding action with third parties[4] on any subject
appertaining to Communication Intelligence except in
accordance with the following understanding:

---

[4]Throughout this agreement third parties are
understood to mean all individuals or authorities
other than those of the United States, the British
Empire, and the British Dominions.

4

TOP SECRET

TOP SECRET

(a) It will be contrary to this agreement to reveal its existence to any third party whatever.

(b) Each party will seek the agreement of the other to any action with third parties, and will take no such action until its advisability is agreed upon.

(c) The agreement of the other having been obtained, it will be left to the party concerned to carry out the agreed action in the most appropriate way, without obligation to disclose precisely the channels through which action is taken.

(d) Each party will ensure that the results of any such action are made available to the other.

6. The Dominions

(a) While the Dominions are not parties to this agreement, they will not be regarded as third parties.

(b) The London SIGINT Board will, however, keep the U. S. informed of any arrangements or proposed arrangements with any Dominion agencies.

(c) STANCIB will make no arrangements with any Dominion agency other than Canadian except through, or with the prior approval of, the London SIGINT Board.

(d) As regards Canada, STANCIB will complete no arrangements with any agency therein without first obtaining the views of the London SIGINT Board.

(e) It will be conditional on any Dominion agencies with whom collaboration takes place that

5

TOP SECRET

TOP SECRET

they abide by the terms of paragraphs 5, 8, and 9 of this agreement and to the arrangements laid down in paragraph 7.

7. Channels Between U. S. and British Empire Agencies

(a) STANCIB will make no arrangements in the sphere of Communication Intelligence with any British Empire agency except through, or with the prior approval of, the London SIGINT Board.

(b) The London SIGINT Board will make no arrangements in the sphere of Communication Intelligence with any U. S. agency except through, or with the prior approval of, STANCIB.

8. Dissemination and Security

Communication Intelligence and Secret or above technical matters connected therewith will be disseminated in accordance with identical security regulations to be drawn up and kept under review by STANCIB and the London SIGINT Board in collaboration. Within the terms of these regulations dissemination by either party will be made to U. S. recipients only as approved by STANCIB; to British Empire recipients and to Dominion recipients other than Canadian only as approved by the London SIGINT Board; to Canadian recipients only as approved by either STANCIB or the London SIGINT Board; and to third party recipients only as jointly approved by STANCIB and the London SIGINT Board.

9. Dissemination and Security - Commercial

STANCIB and the London SIGINT Board will ensure that without prior notification and consent of the other party in each instance no dissemination of information derived from Communication Intelligence sources is made to any individual or agency, governmental or otherwise, that will exploit it for commercial purposes.

6

TOP SECRET

10. Previous Agreements

This agreement supersedes all previous agreements between British and U. S. authorities in the Communication Intelligence field.

11. Amendment and Termination of Agreement

This agreement may be amended or terminated completely or in part at any time by mutual agreement. It may be terminated completely at any time on notice by either party, should either consider its interests best served by such action.

12. Activation and Implementation of Agreement

This agreement becomes effective by signature of duly authorized representatives of the London SIGINT Board and STANCIB. Thereafter, its implementation will be arranged between the Communication Intelligence authorities concerned, subject to the approval of the London SIGINT Board and STANCIB.

For and in behalf of the
London Signal Intelligence Board:

Patrick Marr-Johnson
Colonel, British Army
General Staff

For and in behalf of the
State-Army-Navy Communication Intelligence Board:

Hoyt S. Vandenberg
Lieutenant General, GSC
Senior Member

5 March 1946

7

SECRET

82

TOP SECRET

GLINT

TO BE KEPT UNDER LOCK AND KEY · NEVER TO BE REMOVED
FROM THE OFFICE

USSR.

Ref. No: S/RU-E/T521

Issued: 51/7/48.

Copy No: **206**

FLAG SHIP OF BLACK SEA FLEET TO BE REFITTED
BY MINISTRY OF SHIPBUILDING INDUSTRY, USSR.

From: KAPLUN,
         Deputy Minister, Ministry of Shipbuilding Industry,
         MOSCOW.

To: RASULOV,
         President of the Council of Ministers, Republic of TADZhIKISTAN,
         STALINABAD.

No: Government   5 Jun. 48, 1655.

        By decree of the Council of Ministers of the Union, the
Ministry of Shipbuilding Industry has been charged at very short
notice with the refitting [PEREOBORUDOVAT'] of the flagship of the Black
Sea Fleet. Two PENDI carpets are required, each measuring 270 x 800 cm.
Please give instructions for local cooperation, and if despatch from
stock is not possible, have the carpets made urgently. Please inform
me of your decision. [i]

Comment: [i]   A similar message was addressed to TAShKENT for the
                 President of the UZBEKISTAN Council of Ministers.

Local File No: A/51/89/61.

This is a copy.
The origin...
been retained...
section 3(4) o...
Public Records Act
1958

Signals intelligence reports on deployment of the Soviet Black Sea fleet and the movement of
petroleum products in the Russian Far East, 1948. *HW 75/182*

82

TOP SECRET

GLINT

TO BE KEPT UNDER LOCK AND KEY . NEVER TO BE REMOVED
FROM THE OFFICE

USSR.

Ref. No: S/ARU-E/T322.

Issued: 5/8/48.

Copy No: **206**

DESPATCH OF PETROLEUM PRODUCTS TO FAR EASTERN AND
CENTRAL ASIAN FRONTIER AREAS, USSR.

From: ALYaB'EV,[1]
KRASNOVODSK.

To: BERShITsKIJ,
Chief Directorate of Oil Supply, attached to the State
  Committee of Supply,
MOSCOW.

No: 0230   5 Jul.48.

In June, despatched to others,[ii] in tons :-

Type	Destination[iii]	Quantity
Avtol 10	ULAN UDĒ	170
	GRODEKOVO	387
Avtol 18	ULAN UDĒ	115
	BORZYa	458
	MAN'ChZhURIYa	499
	GRODEKOVO	1220
Diesel Fuel	BORZYa	168
Nigrol	KULTUK	- [iv]
Export Kerosine	KUShKa	3
	Total	2626[v]

FURTHER READING

ALDRICH, Richard, *GCHQ: The Uncensored Story of Britain's Most Secret Intelligence Agency*, Harper Collins, 2011

BRIGGS, Asa, *Secret Days: Code-Breaking in Bletchley Park*, Frontline Books, 2011

COPELAND, Jack, *Turing: Pioneer of the Information Age*, OUP, 2012

KHAN, David, *The Codebreakers*, Weidenfeld & Nicolson, 1974

LEWIN, Ronald, *Ultra Goes to War: The Secret Story*, McGraw Hill, 1978

RICHELSON, Jeffrey, *The Ties that Bind: Intelligence Cooperation between the UKUSA Countries*, Allen & Unwin, 1985

SEBAG-MONTEFIORE, Simon, *Enigma: The Battle for the Code*, Weidenfeld & Nicolson, 2000

SMITH, Michael, *Station X: The Codebreakers of Bletchley Park*, Macmillan, 1998

STRIP, Alan, *Codebreakers in the Far East*, OUP, 1989

WEST, Nigel, *GCHQ: The Secret Wireless War, 1900-1986*, Weidenfeld & Nicolson, 1986

WINTERBOTHAM, Frederick, *The Ultra Secret: The Inside Story of Ultra, Bletchley Park and Enigma*, Weidenfeld & Nicolson, 1974

INDEX

Abwehr, 81-82

Agent Boniface, 83

Agent Snow, 81-82

ARCOS, 41, 43-45

Associated Press, 24

Atlantic, Battle of, 7, 85-95

Austria, annexation of, 42

Automatic Computing Engine (ACE), 116

Barbutt, John, 10

Bell Labs, 115

Bernstorff, Count Johann von, 22

Bletchley Park, 6, 7, 55-65, 80, 83, 85, 87, 90, 92, 96, 99-102, 107, 117

Bombe, 65, 101, 111, 114, 118

Bonaparte, Joseph, 16

Brown, Prime Minister Gordon, 116

Brown, Tommy, 90

BRUSA Agreement, 101

Chicherin, Georgy, 38

Cheltenham, 118

Churchill, Sir Winston, 6, 17, 55, 61, 62, 65, 84, 96, 99, 100, 104, 117

Cold War, 7, 118

Colossus, 61, 115

Comintern, 41, 42

D-Day, 102-04

Daily Herald, 38

Delilah coding machine, 115

Denniston, Alastair, 34, 49, 80, 99, 118

Dollis Hill, 115, 118

Dönitz, Rear Admiral, 87, 88, 92

Dorislaus, Isaac, 10

Eastcote, 107, 118, 119

Elizabeth I, Queen, 6, 10, 13

Enigma machine, 42-54, 56, 60, 85, 88, 91, 99, 101, 111, 114

Fasson, Lieutenant Anthony, 90

Fawcett, Jane, 56

Fetterlein, Ernst, 37

Fish, 65

Flowers, Tommy, 56, 115

Foreign Office, 10, 35, 118

Germany, 22-33, 35
  Navy, 17, 49, 60, 85, 87, 92, 99, 101, 114

Government Code and Cypher School (GC&CS), 6, 34-49, 55, 80, 111

Government Communications Headquarters (GCHQ), 55, 80-82, 117-119

Grazier, Able Seaman Colin, 90

Grey, Nigel de, 56, 118

Hall, Reginald 'Blinker', 22, 24

Hitler, Adolf, 104, 115

Hanslope Park, 82, 115
Hastings, Captain Edward, 101, 118
Holden Agreement, 101

Ismay, Hastings, 61, 65

Japan, 96-102, 106

Knox, Dillwyn, 56, 82, 111
Korean War, 119

Litvinov, Maxim, 38
Lorenz cipher, 6, 56, 65, 66, 115

Magdeburg, SMS, 17, 19-21
Magic, 96, 102
Maltby, Lieutenant Colonel Ted, 82
Mary, Queen of Scots, 11 – 13
Mazinni, Giuseppe, 16
Menzies, Sir Stewart, 49, 82-84, 100
Mexico, 22, 97
Morton, Sir Desmond, 61, 83, 84

Napoleonic Wars, 15
National Archives, Kew, 7, 10
Naval Intelligence Division,
    Admiralty, 17
Nazi Germany, 42, 56, 85, 96, 107
Newman, Max, 65

Official Secrets Act, 7, 34, 37, 83
Operation Claymore, 60-61
Operation, Fortitude, 104-05
Operation Mask, 42
Operation Sealion, 56

Pearl Harbor, 96, 102
Polish Cipher Bureau, 49
Porthcurno, Cornwall, 22

Post Office, Secret Office of, 6, 10, 16
Price, Lieutenant Commander
    Hugh, 87
Purple, 96, 102

Radio Security Service, 81, 115
'Room 40', 7, 23
Rose, Jim, 56
Royal Navy Ships
    HMS *Bulldog*, 60
    HMS *Devonshire, 87, 88*
    HMS *Dorsetshire*, 87
    HMS *Dulverton*, 89
    HMS *Gleaner*, 87
    HMS *Hawarth*, 89
    HMS *Hero*, 89
    HMS *Pakenham*, 89
    HMS *Petard*, 89-91
    HMS *Griffin*, 114

Scovell, George, 15, 17, 18
Secret Intelligence Service (MI6), 35, 56,
    82, 83, 100, 117, 118
Secret Service Committee, 34
Security Service (MI5), 42, 43, 46, 82
Shark, 88, 91, 101
Sinclair, Admiral Hugh, 34, 35, 56, 60
Sinkov, Abraham 'Abe', 96, 99
Soviet Trade Delegation, 38, 41
Soviet Union, 37-48, 118
Standen, Anthony, 8-9
Strachey, Oliver, 82
Sunderland flying boat, 89, 90

Tiltman, Lieutenant Colonel John, 41
Times, The, 16, 38, 116
Travis, Commander Edward 'Jumbo', 80,
    101, 118
Tunny, 65

Turing, Alan, 7, 56, 61, 62, 107-116
Tutte, Bill, 56

U-boats, 22, 60, 85-95
UKUSA Agreement, 118
Ultra, 6, 61, 80, 84, 100-104, 116-118
United States, 22-24, 32, 35, 96, 99, 100,
    101, 116, 118
    Army Signals, 96, 99
    President, 22, 32, 96
    National Security Agency, 119
    Navy, 101, 115

Vienna, Congress of, 16

Wallis, Dr John, 10
Walpole, Sir Robert, 10
Walsingham, Sir Francis, 6, 10
Welchman, Gordon, 56, 61,
    62, 117
Wellington, Duke of, 15
Whaddon Hall, 82
WRENs, 56, 73, 118

Zimmermann telegram, 7, 22-32

Notes

Notes

Notes

Notes

Notes

Notes

Notes

Notes

Notes

Notes

Notes

Notes